Indo-European /a/

BY WILLIAM F. WYATT, JR.

UNIVERSITY OF PENNSYLVANIA PRESS · PHILADELPHIA

Publication of this book has been
made possible by a grant from
the Haney Foundation of the
University of Pennsylvania

Library of Congress Catalog Card Number 73:83140
SBN:8122-7594-2

Printed in the United States of America

Indo-European /a/

Abbreviations

B. Émile Boisacq. Dictionnaire étymologique de la langue grecque. Heidelberg, 1914.

E-M Alfred Ernout and Antoine Meillet. Dictionnaire étymologique de la langue latine. 4th ed. Paris, 1959.

F. Hjalmar Frisk. Griechisches etymologisches Wörterbuch. Heidelberg, 1954–.

IF Indogermanische Forschungen. Berlin.

JAOS Journal of the American Oriental Society. New Haven.

KZ Zeitschrift für vergleichende Sprachforschung. Göttingen.

M. Manfred Mayrhofer. Kurzgefasstes etymologisches Wörterbuch des Altindischen. Heidelberg, 1953–.

P. Julius Pokorny. Indogermanisches etymologisches Wörterbuch. Vol. I. Bern & Munich, 1959.

U. C. C. Uhlenbeck. Kurzgefasstes etymologisches Wörterbuch der Altindischen Sprache. Amsterdam, 1898.

W-H A. Walde. Lateinisches etymologisches Wörterbuch. 3d ed. rev., by J. B. Hofmann. Heidelberg, 1938–1954.

/a/ has always been of central concern to Indo-Europeanists. The first scholars in the last century seriously to attempt the reconstruction of the Indo-European parent tongue derived all the non-high vowels of the European languages, that is to say /e a o/, from an original /a/ which contrasted in Indo-European only with the high vowels /i/ and /u/ in a three-vowel system. Later, as comparative methodology improved, and as the hold of Sanskrit on the minds and hearts of linguists began to weaken, Indo-European /a/ was split up, first into two vowels /e/ and /o/, still nostalgically written a_1 and a_2 by Brugmann in 1876 and de Saussure in 1879; and then finally into four (/e a o/ and the import from the Semitic world, *schwa*). This stage of six short vowels, save for later isolated aberrations, represented the highwater mark of the Indo-European vocalic system, a point from which that system has since been receding. Though /e/ and /o/ together with /i/ and /u/, frequently regarded as the vocalic allophones of /y/ and /w/, have successfully maintained their status as original elements of the vowel system, both /a/ and /ə/ have been expelled by many, /ə/ alone by some.[1] In what follows I shall discuss these displaced vowels, in the hopes of finding a home for at least one of them in our grammars of Indo-European. I shall not be primarily concerned with how they were realized phonetically, but rather with their position in the system, that is to say, with the number of paradigmatic oppositions into which they entered. Did the Indo-European vowel system contain four distinctive vowels to be written /i u e o/ as laryngealists would have it; or five: /i u e o a/, as in Burrow's system; or six, as in the traditional analysis which includes /i u e o a ə/?

The answer to this question of course derives ultimately from an inspection of the data, namely the correspondences between words in the daughter languages. For the sake of simplicity I cite forms only from Greek and Sanskrit: cognates in other languages could easily be cited, but Greek and Sanskrit are here sufficient.[2]

Cognates		*Solutions*		
Greek	*Sanskrit*	*Traditional*	*Laryngeal*	*Burrow*
ἴμεν	imáḥ	i	i	i
ζυγόν	yugám	u	u	u
φέρω	bhárāmi	e	e	e
ὄις	áviḥ	o	e/H_3_	o
ἄγω	ájāmi	a	e/H_2_	a
πατήρ	pitā́	ə	H/C_C	–

Since there are six cognate pairs, there is a maximum of six vowels to be restored to the parent language. Beside the cognates I list the three phonemic solutions to these correspondences which seem to be in the field and worthy of consideration today. The first, the traditional, directly and simply accounts for the correspondences by rewriting one symbol in the protoform with one symbol in the various daughter languages. The laryngeal theory, in one of its less complicated forms, likewise accounts for the correspondences, but by combining two symbols (or phonemes) already in the inventory (namely /H/ and /e/) to provide one of the correspondences: phonetic [a] is phonemic

/H_2e/. /o/ existed in the system also, but I have not given an example of it in the table: /H_2o/ would presumably appear also as [a].[3] Burrow's solution, a five-vowel solution, is more radical and does not directly account for the correspondences.

Burrow (1949) was moved by the small number of correspondences requiring /ə/ to deny /ə/ to Indo-European, not by proving it a variant or development of some other sound, but rather by reanalyzing the correspondences on the basis of which /ə/ was postulated. Thus one of the cornerstones of the doctrine of /ə/, πατήρ = *pitā́* 'father' is removed by assuming (1949:38–39) that both *pitā́* and *duhitā́* 'daughter' (cf. Gk. θυγάτηρ) contain an I-I suffix-*itā*, and thus are to be analyzed etymologically as *p-itā́* and *duh-itā́*, rather than as *pi-tā́* and *duhi-tā́*, the most usual analysis. And in *The Sanskrit Language* (1955:139) he suggests that *pitā́* may contain the weak grade of the root *pā-(y)-* 'to protect.' But whether or not one accepts this etymology, Burrow holds that these words and all others formerly thought by other scholars to contain IE */ə/ contain IE */i/.[4]

Though Burrow's instinct was correct, and though many of his individual arguments are stimulating, nonetheless his main conclusion has rightly found little favor. Denying /ə/ to Indo-European is one thing, but denying the relatedness of the cognates on which it is based is another. In the former case we discard a phoneme, in the latter we discard an entire method together with its body of theory. And yet that is what Burrow in effect has been forced to do. One might as well propose (e.g.) that the /o/ of Gk. γένος 'race' does not correspond directly to the /a/ of Skt. *janaḥ* 'race' because the Skt. form contains a suffix *-aḥ* seen also in *manaḥ* 'mind' and other words, and that therefore the suffix is secondary in *janaḥ*. And this means assuming that only the **gen*-part of the words is related, or in the case of 'father', that only the initial /p/ 's correspond. It is indeed possible, certain in fact, that Sanskrit has occasionally introduced /i/ into positions in which it did not originally appear, but a wholesale substitution of /i/ for Ø in kinship terms (*pitā́*), in participial forms (*sthitáḥ*), and in disyllabic roots (*punīmáḥ*) seems most unlikely. Burrow's solution will not do.

The simplicity of the traditional solution is sufficient recommendation for it, but what of the laryngeal solution with its denial of /a/ to Indo-European (or, in the thinking of some laryngealists, to an earlier stage of it)? Why do laryngealists feel that [a] results from a cluster /H_2e/ and was not a single phoneme? There are various theoretical reasons for this assumption, all deriving from the theory itself and not from the comparative data. These reasons I have discussed in an article in *Language* (Wyatt 1964), and hope to have indicated that they are not sufficient to support the doctrine. But Kuryłowicz (1956 :187–195, 1962: 114) has perhaps most recently expressed what he considers good practical and statistical reasons for adopting the view that [a] = /H_2e/. He points out first that /a/ is distinguished from /o/ in only a few languages, and that /a/ is of secondary origin in the most important cases in those languages. The implication is that /a/ is always of secondary origin. This is of course not a serious argument for his conclusion, but leads up to others which are. [a] tends to appear in words of concrete character which do not in general belong to the basic vocabulary, words like *goose bean nose salt*. Few words of this type can be connected with verbal roots, most appear in nonablauting paradigms, and borrowings from *a/o*-languages into *o*-languages (and vice-versa) may well have played a role in causing us to reconstruct an /a/ where we should reconstruct /o/. Third, the other side of the same coin, [a] does not occur in pronouns, numerals, names of parts of the body, kinship terms—thus not in the basic vocabulary. Both these statements concerning the distribution of /a/ in the vocabulary are correct, but they do not really prove anything. It would be pleasant to think that we are able to explain why the IE languages did not utilize [a] in pronouns, etc., but we cannot, and we might with as much justification object to the doctrine of /H_2/ that /H_2e/ does not occur in pronouns, etc. We cannot in general explain the absence of a tendency or artifact.

The fourth criterion is the most important, and so far as I know is original with Kuryłowicz. Neither he nor anyone else denies the validity of correspondences involving initial [a] such as: Skt. *ájati* 'drives', Gk. ἄγω 'lead'; Skt. *ájraḥ* 'field', Gk. ἀγρός 'field'; Skt. *ákṣaḥ* 'axle', Gk. ἄξων 'axle'. But, says Kuryłowicz (1956:189), if the [a] reconstructed from these forms and others were really a separate phoneme /a/, we should expect to find ten times as many instances of it in the interior of the word as initially: words with an initial vowel constitute only about 10 per cent of the IE vocabulary. We should then expect to find some 220 or 230 roots with internal /a/, but in fact find only about thirty. This, according to Kuryłowicz, proves that /a/ did not exist as a separate entity in Indo-European, and that the initial correspondences are to be analyzed otherwise, the otherwise being /H_2e/ in keeping with the doctrine that all IE words began with a consonant, and that every verbal root contained the /e/ vocalism. Thus /H_2ego:/ becomes precisely parallel to /lego:/, /bhero:/, and so forth.

But are these figures and percentages corroborative of the conclusion they are meant to support? Frequency of phonemic occurrence is likely to be erratic in any event (Szemerényi 1964:9), and one need look no further than Latin in his search for languages with relatively frequent initial /a/ but /a/ rare internally (in noninitial syllables). But to stay closer to Indo-European, suppose one were to apply the same calculations to nonapophonic /e/ and /o/, that is to say to /e/ that does not alternate morphophonemically with /o/, and /o/ that does not alternate morphophonemically with /e/. Surely he would find almost exactly the same situation: a number of /e/ and /o/ appearing initially in very well attested roots, but next to no such cognate sets internally.[5] And yet no one would wish to deny /e/ and /o/ to Indo-European. Kuryłowicz's argument is not compelling, but endeavoring to account for the distribution of [a] which he stresses leads one to another conclusion which both elucidates his observation and leads to a proper appreciation of the IE vowel system.

Indo-European [ə] has almost precisely the opposite distribution from [a]. It never occurs initially, but is extremely frequent in the interior of a word, generally unaccented. It seems indicated, on the basis of the distribution of [a] and [ə] to join them in one protophoneme which appeared as [a] initially, but which was raised (or weakened) to [ə] in the interior of the word, at least in Indo-Iranian. I offer the hypothesis that [a] and [ə] are allophones of one original phoneme which we may write /a/. There were then five oppositions in the IE vowel system, oppositions which can be best represented by the phonemes /i u e o a/, the vowels, that is, which are found later on in Latin, Greek, Celtic, and Armenian.

There are a number of prima facie reasons which tend

to support the assumption that [a] and [ə] were originally members of the same phoneme.

1) First, Indo-Iranian is the only branch of the IE family to show a distinct reflex of [ə]: all others show the same reflex of [a] and [ə]. This fact might tend to suggest that Indo-Iranian has innovated in this matter, a suggestion rendered the more likely by the fact that Indo-Iranian is also the only language group to show a merger of /e/ and /a/, a merger which might well have involved only the accented or lower allophones of /a/. The merger may be displayed as follows:

/i/		/u/				
	[ə]		⟶	/i/ [ə] /u/	⟶	/i/ /u/
/e/		/o/		/e/ [a] /o/		/a/
	[a]					

That is to say, an original IE system of three distinctive vocalic levels was collapsed into a two-level system. Upon the merger of all low vowels, [ə], the higher allophone of /a/, was split off from /a/, and, because it was a high vowel, merged with /i/.

2) Second, from a purely IE point of view, we are led to reconstruct six short vowel oppositions if we include schwa, and only five long vowel oppositions. We might rather expect either the same number of oppositions (as in Latin), or fewer short than long (as in Greek). The laryngeal theory, to be sure, handles this asymmetry easily by assuming that [ə] is merely the vocalic allophone of /H/.

3) As Kuryłowicz and others have pointed out, and as I have already mentioned, [a] is rare internally in the word, but frequent initially. This fact should indicate that /a/ appears in another guise in the interior of a word. And since [ə] never occurs initially, it seems indicated to assume

that [a] and [ə] are different allophones of the same phoneme. We shall attempt a more formal proof of this hypothesis later on.

The idea that [a] and [ə] are variants of the same phoneme is far from new. De Saussure in fact suggested it back in 1879, though his pronouncements on the subject are not altogether clear.[6] As is well known, he established for Indo-European two new 'coefficients sonantiques' *A* and *o̯* which combined with /e o/ to yield /ē ā ō/ (<eA, oA; <eA, oA; <eo̯, oo̯ respectively) just as /i/ and /u/ combined with these same vowels to yield /ei oi eu ou/. *A*, for we may omit *o̯* here, between consonants and initially is continued in all the daughter languages by /a/ (or its continuation /o/) (1922:110). Thus *Ag* yields Lat. *ágo,* Gk. ἄγω, Skt. *ájati.* But under certain other conditions it appeared as ^{A}, and it was this ^{A} which accounts for the correspondence Skt. *sthitáḥ,* Gk. στατός, Lat. *status* where we find Skt. /i/ = Eur. /a/ rather than /a/ = /a/ (1922: 110–111): 'On pourra donc sans crainte établir la règle que, lorsque les langues européennes ont *A*, en syllabe ouverte comme en syllabe fermée l'arien montre *a bref.* Mais ceci veut dire simplement que l'*a* n'est pas un *a* long: il arrive en effet que dans certaines positions, par example à la fin des racines, ce n'est plus du tout un *a*, mais bien *i* ou *ī*, au moins en sanskrit, qui se trouve placé en regard du phonème *A* des langues d'Europe.' And further (1922: 226): 'Nous avons reconnu dans ce dernier (sc. Skt. /i/ in *sthitáḥ*) le descendant d'une voyelle faible proethnique désignée par ^{A}, voyelle qui n'est elle-même qu'une modification de l'espèce d'*a*, ou des espèces d'*a* autres que a_1 et a_2 (*A* o̯).' And (1922:167): 'Nous croyons que cette voyelle était une *espèce d'e muet, provenant de l'altération des phonèmes A et o̯.*' He was quite insistent on the fact that this ^{A} arose

from a full vowel (1922:167): 'Dire que la voyelle faible proethnique d'où dérive l'*i* de *sthitá, çistá,* n'a point été d'abord une voyelle pleine serait renoncer à expliquer l'*ā* de *sthā́man, çā́sti,* dont elle forme la seconde partie.' He was not clear, though, as to what brought about the alteration of the phonemes *A* and *o* to ^{A}. He simply states (1922:167, 141) that this change was general at the end of roots, partial in roots ending in a consonant. He explicitly denies (1922:166) that the position of the accent could explain the change completely, though he did agree that accented *A* appeared always as Skt. /a/. What was needed at this point was an analysis of the distribution of *A* showing under what conditions it passed to Skt. /a/ and under what conditions it passed to /i/. This de Saussure did not provide.

De Saussure also posited two origins for his *A*, and it was the origin of *A*, and not its nature, which prevented later scholars from accepting his ideas. He maintained that the /ī/ of the weak forms of Skt. ninth-class verbs (*punīmáḥ* 'we cleanse') and the /i/ of the agent nouns (*pavitár*) were phonologically identical with the /i/ of *sthitáḥ:* all of these /i/ derive from ^{A}, which in turn derives from *A*. But the ^{A} of the ninth-class verbs stems from an original full-grade vowel, while the ^{A} of *sthitáḥ* is the reduction of a long /ā/(1922:226): 'D'autre part il y a entre l'*ĭ* ou ^{A} de *sthitá, pītá,* et l'ī̆ ou ^{A} de *pavi-, grabhī,* cette importante différence morphologique, que le premier résulte de la réduction d'un *ā* (a_1A), tandis que le second paraît exister de fondation à l'état autophtongue. S'il se combine avec a_1, dans le présent en -*nā*, il n'en préexistait pas moins à ce présent'. Thus some IE *A* are reductions of /ā/ (< **eA*), while others are vowels *A* quite on par with /e o/. The type represented by *Ag-* with *A* in initial position de Saussure considered to be a weakening of /ā/ (1922:150). A schematic representation of de Saussure's ideas would show (1922:164ff.):

I		II			III
a (<eA)			A		A>/a/ (generally)
	>A	A>			
			A	A	
A					>/i/ (at the end of roots)

The reason for de Saussure's assumption that the A of ninth-class verbs was an original vowel and not also the weakening of /ā/ was a morphological one. In Skt. seventh-class verbs there occurs an alternation *-na-* ~ *-n-*, e.g. in *yunákti* ~ *yuñjmáḥ* 'join'. De Saussure felt that these forms were to be analyzed as root + *-ne-* ~ *-n-* + ending (*yu-ná-k-ti* ~ *yu-ñ-j-máḥ*) and not root + *-n-* + ending (*yu-n-ák-ti* ~ *yu-ñ-j-máḥ*). In other words the ablaut variation affected the infix and not the root, and the root remained constant throughout as *yuj-*. He felt that the same *-ne-* ~ *-n-* occurred also in fifth- and ninth-class verbs, in the shapes *-ne-u-* ~ *-n-u-* (*stṛṇóti* ~ *stṛṇumáḥ*) 'strew' and *-ne-A-* ~ *-n-A* (*punā́ti* ~ *punīmáḥ*) 'cleanse' respectively. And since the root form appears as such in the plural with only a nasal infixed, the root forms of these verbs must have been *stru-* and *puA-*. If so, the /ā/ of ninth-class singulars must have resulted from the contraction of *-ne-* and *-A-*, two vowels. In this case, then, the vocalism of the weak forms is original, and that of the strong forms secondary. In the case of *stā-* ~ *stA-*, *stā-* (<**steA-*) was original and *stA-* (<**stā-*) secondary.

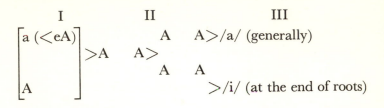

The doctrine of the original full-grade vowel *A* was only so strong as the analysis of nasal-infix verbs, and some scholars could not accept de Saussure's views. Thus Streitberg (1915:208) favored analyzing these words as more literally nasal-infix verbs: i.e. verbs with only a nasal infixed, and concluded that *punā́ti*:*punīmáḥ* were to be analyzed: *pu-n-ā́-ti*:*pu-n-ī-máḥ*, in which event *-ī-* again could be interpreted as the reduction of *-ā-*: 'Man kann jedoch mit gleichem Rechte auch folgende Trennung vornehmen: **bhi-n-éd-mi*, **pu-n-ā́-mi*, **kᵛi-n-éu-mi*. Bei dieser Auffassung existiert das auslautende *i* der *sēṭ*-Wurzeln nicht *de fondation à l'état autophtongue* (S. 242), sondern ist das Ergebnis der Reduktion einer betonten Länge, ist also wie das *i* von *sthi-ta-* zu beurteilen'. Thus all *A* are to be regarded as the reduction of /ā/.

The notion that *A* was the product of the reduction of an unaccented long vowel also caused trouble for de Saussure. Hübschmann (1885:1ff., 65ff., 1900:27–28) quite correctly pointed out—something known already to de Saussure—that long vowels were reduced only in unaccented syllables, and that therefore there should be no cases of accented *A* (1900:28): 'Bestand aber ein hochtoniges idg. á (=skr. a, griech. a), das natürlich weder mit dem hochtonigen idg. ā́ = éạ (=skr. ā, griech. ā) noch mit dem daraus (in unbetonter Silbe!) entstandenen ą (ə) identische sein konnte, so muss an diesem *a* das ganze System de Saussure's scheitern, das allen Ablaut auf den Wechsel von o:e:—zurückführen will. Denn idg. ág¹ō kann weder = óag¹ō noch éag¹ō noch -agṓ sein.'[7] But of course there are cases of accented [a]. For these Hübschmann reserved the symbol *a*, and symbolized the reduced long vowel by *ə*. He was the first to my knowledge to posit the two sounds as distinct phonemic entities.

It is well at this point to emphasize again the fact that Hübschmann was talking about the origin of *A* and not its nature, and concluded something about its nature from its origin. It is of course quite possible for a single sound to result from the merger of two quite clearly distinct earlier sounds, and arguments about the origins of sounds have no place in discussions concerning their nature. What Hübschmann in fact did was to establish two morphophonemes, *a* and *ə*, morphophonemes which enable one to infer the ablaut series to which the form in question belongs: forms with *ə* always have beside them other forms with a long vowel, while those with *a* do not, at least not necessarily. This may indeed by a useful sort of convention, but it has nothing to do with the more or less phonemic analysis of reconstructed systems.

Bechtel next took up de Saussure's idea (1892:240 ff.), and endeavored to get around Hübschmann's objections to it by positing an intermediate stage *a* in the development from *ā* to *ə*. He, too, accepted de Saussure's position that there was no original IE accented *a*, and that *ə* was merely the result of unaccented *a*. But he added an accent shift to the picture (1892:252): 'So drängt sich die Vermutung auf, dass das arische *a* überhaupt nicht durch das folgende *y*, sondern durch den Accent bedingt sei, der in Folge späteren Verschiebung das *a* zu einer Zeit getroffen habe, als die Verwandlung des arischen *a* in *i* noch nicht vollzogen war'. He thus still held to the doctrine that *a* arose only from the reduction of an original long vowel. His view can be represented schematically:

1) ā > a
2) Some *a* receive the accent
3) á > a
   a > ə (Skt. i ~ ī)

Though Bechtel's assumption of an intermediate stage *a* should have freed him from attacks based on the origin of *a*, that is, on questions of ablaut series, he was nonetheless so attacked,[8] and it remained for Pedersen (1900:75–86) finally to free the question from its ablaut bondage. Pedersen quite clearly and correctly saw that (1900:75) the different ablaut series can prove only that /a/ had several sources, not that it had two different pronunciations. And since Indo-Iranian is alone in showing a divergent development of *a* and *ə* (1900:76): 'so bleibt nur zu untersuchen, ob die doppelheit *i*:*a* auf arischen boden durch ein speziell arisches lautgesetz entstanden sein kann. Falls eine solche möglichkeit existiert, ist jede andere erklärung abzulehnen; besteht die möglichkeit eines arischen lautgesetz nicht, so darf auf eine idg. doppelheit geschlossen werden.' With ablaut considerations resolutely banished from the field, only phonological equations were considered. And on the basis of purely phonological evidence Pedersen concluded (1900:85): 'ein unbetontes idg. *a* in offener (nicht auf sonorlaut ausgehender) silbe geht im Arischen in *i* über, wenn es weder im anlaut noch im auslaut steht, nicht auf *y v k* (*g*) folgt und nicht unmittelbar vor *y* steht.'

Pedersen's views have found little favor. Brugmann (1904:80), without arguing the matter, simply states that he is unconvinced; Hirt (1900:148–149) demonstrated that the rule that *a* does not pass to *i* after *v* is contravened by Skt. *tavā́ḥ* 'strong' but *taviṣáḥ* 'id.'; and Güntert (1916) devoted some twenty pages to a detailed attack on Pedersen's formulation. But Pedersen attempted to establish his opinion further (1905:398–402), included it in his discussion of Semitic affinities of IE (1907:349), and maintained it still in his large Celtic grammar (1909:30). So far as I know he never gave it up, though he did modify it in one important regard (1926:27), as we shall see below.

And it is clear that certain aspects of Pedersen's formulation are incorrect or unnecessary. Preceding /y/ can have had nothing to do with the preservation of /a/. The rule is in the first place unnecessary because needed to account only for the two correspondences: Skt. *yátati* 'attach', Gk. *ζητέω* 'seek' and Skt. *yájati* 'worship', Gk. *ἅζομαι* 'stand in awe of'. But the first of these equations must be discarded (see App. II †26), and the /a/ of the Skt. form in the second equation is sufficiently accounted for by the accent. Furthermore there are counterexamples which show that the Skt. outcome of IE */ya/ was something other than /ya/. Güntert (1916: 6–7) mentions *jītá* < *jyā-* 'overpower', Gk. *βιάω* 'constrain' and *pīná* < *pyā-* 'fill up'. To these can be added the internal Skt. evidence of words like *ī́psati* 'wishes to obtain', the desiderative of *āp-* in *āpnóti* 'obtains'. There are also the excellent cognate pairs: Skt. *bharantī*, Gk. *φέρουσα* < **bherontia* 'carrying (fem. part.); Skt. *trī*, Gk. *τρία* < **tria* 'three (ntr. plur.)'; Skt. *krītáḥ* 'bought', Gk. *πριατός* < **k^{w}riatós*. All these words show that IE*/ia/ (or /ya/) passes to /i:/ in Skt.

A preceding semivowel can have had no effect on the preservation of /a/. Nor can a preceding /k/. It is indeed interesting and significant that /a/ appears with some frequency in initial syllables after /k/ and that [ə] does not, but this fact has more to do with the question of the IE gutturals than with the IE vocalic system. /a/ > [ə] after the other velar consonants (Pedersen 1900: 77–78) and it is unreasonable to suppose that the voiceless velar had an effect on the succeeding phoneme not shared by its voiced and aspirated counterparts. Hence we must strip Pedersen's formulation at least of the conditioning effect of the preceding phoneme: we shall reserve judgment on the other aspects of his formulation till after we have examined the evidence.

Later scholars seem by and large to have retained Hübschmann's view of the IE vowel system, however they may differ in their interpretation of it, and to have ignored Pedersen's view. I presume that the reason for this neglect of Pedersen is that many scholars felt that Güntert's criticisms were sufficient to destroy his position, and that furthermore some scholars at least felt that the laryngeal theory, buttressed anew by the evidence of Hittite, provided a more powerful explicatory device. In any event, the more traditionally-minded Indo-Europeanists, such as Krahe (1962:54), retain both /a/ and /ə/. Laryngealists are split into two camps on the question. The more orthodox view holds that [a] arises from /H_2e/ (and /H_4e/ for those who accept /H_4/), while [ə] develops from any /H/ between consonants. A somewhat radical view maintains that there was no schwa in Indo-European and that consonantal /H/ did not develop to vocalic schwa. Those who subscribe to this view (Burrow 1949) derive [a] from /H_2e/ in some cases, and also from /a/. I propose in what follows to examine the evidence for IE /a/ and schwa, in hopes of providing an acceptable proof that IE [a] and [ə] are allophones of the same phoneme, and that /a/ developed to [ə] only under certain conditions.

I. According to Pedersen's view IE */a/ in absolute initial position appears as /a/ everywhere. To support this view he gave (1900:76–77) Brugmann's list (1897:158–163).

1. Skt. *ájati* 'drives', Gk. *ἄγω* 'lead' (M. I.23, F. I.18).
2. Skt. *ájraḥ* 'field', Gk. *ἀγρός* 'field' (M. I.23, F. I.16).
3. Skt. *ákṣaḥ* 'axle', Gk. *ἄξων* 'id.' (M. I.16, F. I.116).
4. Skt. *ápa* 'away, off', Gk. *ἀπό* 'from' (M. I.37, F. I.122).
5. Skt. *ánti* 'before', Gk. *ἀντί* 'id.' (M. I.36, F. I.113–114).
6. Skt. *áśmā* 'stone', Gk. *ἄκμων* 'anvil' (M. I.60, F. I.54).
7. Skt. *catur-aśráḥ* 'four-cornered', Gk. *ἄκρος* 'end' (M. I.61, F. I.59–60).

8. Skt. *áṁhaḥ* 'anxiety', Gk. ἄγχω 'press tight' (M. I.14, F. I.17–18).
9. Skt. *áyaḥ* 'iron, metal', Lat. *aes* 'copper' (M. I.46, W-H I.19–20).
10. Skt. *ániti* 'breathes', Gk. ἄνεμος 'wind', Lat. *animus* 'mind' (M. I.33, F. I.105, W-H I.49–50).
11. Skt. *amláḥ* 'sour', Lat. *amārus* 'bitter' (M. I.46, W-H I.35).

To this list Pedersen himself adds:

12. Skt. *áśru* 'tear', Gk. δάκρυ 'id.' (M. I.60, F. I.344).
13. Skt. *argháḥ* 'worth', Gk. ἀλφάνω 'acquire' (M. 50, F. I.81).
14. Skt. *ásṛk* 'blood', Lat. *asser* 'blood' (M. I.66, W-H I.72).

Still more examples are provided by Kuryłowicz (1956: 187–188):

15. Skt. *áṅkaḥ* 'curve', Gk. ἄγκος 'bend' (M. I.19, F. I.10–12).
16. Skt. *ajáḥ* 'he-goat', OIr. *ag* 'cow, deer' (P. 6–7, M. I.23).
17. Skt. *ánu* 'after', Gk. ἀνά 'up' (M. I.34, F. I.100).
18. Skt. *ándhaḥ* 'herb', Gk. ἄνϑος 'flower' (M. I.36, F. I.108–109).
19. Skt. *aráḥ* 'spoke of a wheel', Gk. ἀραρίσκω 'join' (M. I.48, F. I.128–129).
20. Skt. *árjunaḥ* 'shining', Gk. ἀργός 'id.' (M. I.50–51, F. I.132–133).
21. Skt. *árdati* 'flows', Gk. ἄρδω 'water (cattle)' (M. I.51, F. I.135).
22. Skt. *áva* 'down, off', Lat. *au-* 'away' (M. I.56, W-H I.79).
23. Skt. *āyúḥ* 'living', Gk. αἰών 'life' (M. I.77, F. I.49).

24. Skt. *āvíḥ* 'openly', Gk. ἀΐω 'perceive' (M. I.82, F. I.48–49).
25. Skt. *éṣati* 'seeks', Arm. *aiç̣* 'enquête' (M. I.130, 85).
26. Skt. *énaḥ* 'crime', Gk. αἴνυμαι 'take' (M. I.128, F. I.41).
27. Skt. *édhaḥ* 'fuel', Gk. αἴθω 'kindle' (M. I.128, F. I.37–38).
28. Skt. *ójaḥ* 'strength', Gk. αὐξάνω 'increase' (M. I.131, F. I.187–188).

Most of these comparisons are sound and can be retained, but the list must nonetheless be pared down a bit. *áśru* cannot be included because the question of its initial vowel is not securely answered, and the precise relation of *áśru* to Gk. δάκρυ, Lat. *lacrima,* etc. is uncertain. Though Szemerényi (1964:8) counts this correspondence as sure, Kuryłowicz (1956:194) does not include it in his list of forms pointing to IE */a/, and considers δάκρυ a 'European word'. Much the same difficulty arises with *ásṛk,* the initial vowel of which is rendered uncertain by Gk. ἔαρ (εἶαρ, ἦαρ) and Hitt. *esḫar* (F. I.432). *āyúḥ* and *āvíḥ* must be excluded from the list because they show a correspondence /a:/ = /a/, not /a/ = /a/. Though it is likely that the forms are in fact related morphologically, they cannot be used for comparisons on the phonological level. The same must be said of *árdati* : ἄρδω, for the vowel in the Gk. form is long (Herodian 2.109, F. I.135). Perhaps also, in view of Frisk's criticisms (1938:8–12), it is best to give up the connection of *énaḥ* and Gk. αἴνυμαι.

Numerous forms remain, however, enough to show that an */a/ must be reconstructed for Indo-European in initial syllables. As Kuryłowicz says (1956:189), one cannot cast doubt on these correspondences without contesting the very principles of comparative linguistics. We can therefore establish the rule that some IE */a/ appear in initial position as /a/ both in the European languages and in Indo-Iranian as well. Pedersen felt that all IE */a/ in initial position remained in all languages, but he may have been overenthusiastic. If we look again at the now somewhat shorter list of cognates, we find that almost all the Skt. forms have the /a/ accented. The suspicion therefore arises that perhaps only accented IE */a/- (or accented I-I */a/-) appears as /a/ in Indo-Iranian, and that the reflex of unaccented */a/ is something else. The only counterexamples to such a narrower formulation of the rule are: *catur-aśráḥ; ajáḥ, ajínam; aráḥ; argháḥ; amláḥ,* five examples out of twenty-two. And whereas accented */a/- occurs in etymologically unexceptionable morphemes, some of the correspondences displaying unaccented */a/- are questionable.

catur-aśráḥ, however, is probably related to *ἄκρος* in appearance only. Wackernagel (1905:119), followed by Mayrhofer (M. I.61), felt that *-aśráḥ* is not a form inherited as such from Indo-European, but rather is the regular replacement of *áśriḥ* in composition. Now *áśriḥ* is most likely to be related to Gk. *ἄκρις* 'hill-top' (M. I.61, F. I.59–60, Kuryłowicz 1956:188), and hence rather supports than contradicts the rule that only accented IE */a/- passes to Ind. /a/. But it is possible also that *áśriḥ* is rather to be compared with Gk. *ὄκρις* 'jagged point', Lat. *ocris* 'mons confragosus', in which event it is irrelevant to the discussion at hand (F. I.59–60, II.374; W-H II.199).

There are difficulties also with the equation Skt. *amláḥ* 'sour', Lat. *amārus* 'bitter', PGmc. **ampra-* < **ambro-*'sour, bitter', and Kuryłowicz does not even mention it in his list (1956:188). In the first place the Skt. form is not attested until fairly late, being epic and classical only (Wackernagel 1954:862), and secondly it never occurs in an accented text, so that we cannot be sure of the accentuation (Birwé

1956:198). *amláḥ* therefore lacks the secure credentials one hopes for in Skt. words. And there are formal difficulties. Frisk (1934:14) includes this word among formations in *-ro-* which show good semantic agreement but 'slight formal discrepancies'. He is, however, inclined to accept the equation, though he is uncertain about Lat. *amārus,* saying that if it is related, it must have been refashioned on some unknown model. The difficulty is that the earliest Germanic form reconstructable is **ampra-* which could develop from **ambro-* with a *-b-*. But the Skt. forms *amláḥ* and *ambláḥ* (Lex.) presumably must derive from a form without *-b-*, such as **am-ro-*. And the Lat. form not only lacks a *-b-*, but has a long vowel between the *-m-* and the *-r-*. One could indeed assume an original **amro-* continued directly by Sanskrit, but with epenthetic *-b-* in Germanic, but the Lat. form still proves recalcitrant.

There is also difficulty with the initial vowel. In addition to Skt. *amláḥ* and Lat. *amārus,* the following forms are usually cited as cognate:[9] Alb. *tamlë* '(saure) Milch', *ambëlë, ëmblë* 'süss', *tëmblë* 'Galle' (with the /t/- being an article); PGmc. **ampra-*; OIr. *om* 'raw', W. *of* 'id.'; Lett. *amuols* 'Sauerklee'. As can be seen from the list, even if we assume that all these forms are indeed related, only two languages, Latin and the Celtic languages, can give any evidence as to the quality of the original vowel, and that evidence is contradictory. Celtic points to original */o/, Latin, to original */a/. Pedersen (1909:32) felt that OIr. *om* contains the original vocalism, and that Lat. *amārus* has a secondary /a/. The original IE root form was therefore */om/-. Pokorny seems to agree (777–778), for he lists all the forms under **om-*, and not **am-*. None of this proves the assumption of an IE **am-ro* wrong, but makes rather more likely a form such as **om(a)-ro* as starting-point for the developments in the daughter languages.

Skt. *ajáḥ* 'he-goat', *ajā́* 'she-goat' also contravene my

rule, though they are in accord with Pedersen's, if, that is, they are cognate with OIr. *ag*. And, though *ag* is generally connected with Skt. *ahī́* 'cow', Ave. *azī* 'pregnant', and not with *ajáḥ* (M. I.68), it seems most likely that Kuryłowicz is right in connecting it rather with *ajáḥ*. In addition to *ag*, the family of *ajáḥ* includes: Lith. *ožỹs* 'he-goat', *ožkà* 'she-goat'; Alb. *dhī* (< **agī*) 'she-goat'; and more impressively: Skt. *ajínam* 'skin'; Lith. *ožìnis* 'zum Ziegenbock gehörig': OCS (*j*)*azno* < **azъno* 'skin'. But the Slavic and Lith. forms must be removed from consideration on the phonological level, for all forms in these languages point to an original */a:g/-, not */ag/-: only Alb. *dhī*, OIr. *ag* and Skt. *ajā́*, *ajáḥ* point to */ag/-. And the suffix differs in each of these languages: OIr. *-es*; Skt. *-ā*, *-os*; Alb. *-ī*. Hence they cannot all derive from one and the same ancestral word. The best that can be said for them is that they all derive from a single root-noun **ag-*, homophonous with the verbal root **ag-* 'drive, lead', originally identical with it, and of course since monosyllabic, originally accented. Thus all the forms in the daughter languages are derivatives of */ag/- formed independently, all meaning 'the driven one', a meaning applied to goats in Albanian and Sanskrit, but to cows in Old Irish. There is, so far as I can see, no reason to assume with Thieme (1953:580–581) an IE word **ag* 'goat', and there is of course still less reason to posit an IE word **agós* 'goat' ancestral to Skt. *ajáḥ*.

The other two cases, *argháḥ,* and *aráḥ,* though clearly counter-examples, and though almost certainly cognate with European forms with initial /a/, are not sufficient to destroy the rule. Though the forms are cited in these shapes, accented derivatives of the same roots do occur in Sanskrit, and we may presume, faute de mieux, that it was these accented forms (or other accented derivatives now lost) that preserved the /a/, unless indeed we assume an accent shift within Indic. In the case of *argháḥ* there occur *árjati* 'acquires' and *árhati* 'is worth', and for *aráḥ: áram* 'readily, enough'; the regular unaccented form of this root is seen in *ṛtáḥ* 'right, true'. Hence we may reformulate Pedersen's rule to read : IE /á/ remains initially in all IE languages.

The rule just given seems unexceptionable as stated, but one wonders what happens to unaccented /a/, and also how one is to account for cases for which scholars have in the past been tempted to reconstruct /ə/ in initial position. There are three classes of examples which are relevant here, each with its own problems, and each of which must be dealt with, however cursorily, before my rule can be considered ready for serious consideration. 1) A Skt. form like *ī́psati* 'wishes to obtain' (instead of **yapsati*) from *āpnóti* favors an analysis **iəpseti* (or **iHpsati*) over **iapseti:* */ya/ should appear as /ya/ in Sanskrit, as in *yájate*, rather than as /i:/. 2) The Gk. prothetic vowel, seen in ἀνήρ 'man' as opposed to Skt. *nṛ* 'id.' again might demand an analysis **Hner* or **əner* with the rule that */H/ or */ə/ passed to /a/ in Greek but to Ø in Sanskrit (and elsewhere): without this rule one might expect Skt. **anṛ* instead of *nṛ*. 3) Even if this /a/ = Ø correspondence be attributed to a literally prothetic vowel in Greek, we nevertheless find correspondences, such as Lat. *aurora*, Lith. *aušrà*, Skt. *uṣáḥ* 'dawn' in which all European languages show /a/, while Indo-Iranian alone shows no vowel at all. Again one is inclined to reconstruct something other than **aus-* as the IE form, possibly **əus-*, on the assumption that, though IE */a/>/a/ everywhere, IE */ə/>Eur. /a/ but Skt. Ø. We shall take up these difficulties one by one.

1) The first of these difficulties was raised by Güntert (1916:5–6) as an objection to Pedersen's view that IE initial */a/ remains in Sanskrit. He held that the following

countercases are sufficient to invalidate Pedersen's rule:

ī́psati 'wishes to obtain', desiderative to √ā̄p in *āpnóti* 'obtain' <**i* + *əp* + *se-* (M. I.95).

ī́kṣate 'sees', a reduplicated present to the *akṣ-* seen in *akṣi* 'eye' <**i* + *ək* + *se-* (M. I.95).

dvīpáḥ 'island', a compound of *dvi-* + the weak form of *ā́paḥ* 'water' <**dwi* + *əp-* (M. II.86–87).

ī́hate 'desires', connected with Ave. *āziš* 'Begierde', and perhaps further with Gk. ἀχήν 'needy', hence from **i* + *əgh-* (M. I.97, F. I.200).

Güntert reasons (1916:6): 'diese Fälle sind gewichtig genug um die Unhaltbarkeit der Behauptung, *i* = europ. *a* begegne niemals im Anfang arischer Worte, zu erweisen.'

But in fact these cases are not relevant to Pedersen's rule at all. They show that IE */a/ could appear in Sanskrit as something other than /a/ in morpheme initial position, but have no bearing whatsoever on the question of the fate of IE */a/ in word-initial position. They do, however, indicate that IE */a/ (and */o/ in *ī́kṣate*)[10] when unaccented (cf. *yáj-*: II.43 below), and when not protected by accented forms elsewhere in the paradigm, appeared in Sanskrit as length after /i/ (and /u/ as well: cf. *anūpáḥ* 'situated near the water'). This distributional statement will later prove to hold in all positions in the word. Hence unaccented IE /a/ disappears after a semivowel with compensatory lengthening of that semivowel: unaccented /a/>/:/

$$/\begin{bmatrix} \mathrm{i} \\ \mathrm{u} \end{bmatrix}\underline{\qquad}\ \mathrm{C}.$$

2) The prothetic vowel in Greek is a large and complicated problem, too complicated in fact to be used as evidence of a contrast between /a/ and /ə/ (/H/) in initial position. Nonetheless it has been so used, and in particular in cases like Gk. ἀνήρ, Skt. *nṛ* 'man'; Gk. ὄνομα, Skt. *nāma*

(Arm. *anun*) 'name'. From these words scholars have concluded that IE */əR/ (or /HR/) contrasting with /aR/ (or /H_2eR/) developed to *VR*- in Greek (and Armenian) but to *ØR*- elsewhere.

Prothesis is, however, too regular, and at that too regular in terms of purely Gk. phonological conditioning, to allow for such a conclusion. In the first place, as is well known, */r/- always receives a prothetic vowel in Greek, and relevant instances can therefore be found only before /l m n w/ (there are no cases before /y/). Furthermore, even before /l m n w/ prothesis occurs only, though not always, in two major categories of words: 1) before a resonant followed by /e/ in a closed syllable; and before /a/ in either an open or a closed syllable, a position in which there is variation between forms with prothesis and forms without: 2) as the result of the analogical extension of a syllabic resonant to positions in the paradigm where the resonant was consonantal. These two environments may be exemplified in the first instance by a mere listing, in the second by a concrete example (examples from Lejeune 1955:127–129, 148):

a)	ἀλείφω	but	λούω
	ἐλεύθερος		λόξος
	ἀλείτης		λείπω (λέλοιπα, ἔλιπον)
	ἀμέλγω	but	μήτηρ
	ὀμείχω		μέλι
	ὄνειδος	but	νέος
	ἀνεψιός		νέφος
	ἐλαχύς	beside	λαχεῖα
	ἀμαλός		μαλακός
	ἐέλδεται	beside	ἔλδεται
	ἐέρση		ἕρση

The quality of the vowel varied, apparently in terms both of the following consonant and of the succeeding vowel or diphthong.

b) The prothetic vowel in *ἀνήρ* is the result of a leveling of the irregular paradigm */né:r/, */arós/ by extension of the /a/ (</n/) of the oblique cases to the nominative and accusative cases: thereupon the stem of the word was taken to be /an/-, and this /an/- was introduced to the oblique cases. The original IE paradigm of this word in the singular was (restricting myself to cases preserved in Greek):

/né:r/ /nrós/ /nrí/ /nérm/

From this there developed in Greek, after the vocalization of the sonant resonants, the paradigm:

/né:r/ /aṛós/ /arí/ /néra/

This irregular paradigm was leveled by introducing /a/ to the nominative and accusative:

/ané:r/ /arós/ /arí/ /anéra/

whereupon /an/- formed the base of the paradigm and was extended to the oblique cases, and the classical paradigm resulted:[11]

/ané:r/ /andrós/ /andrí/ /anéra/

There never was a vocalic element preceding the initial */n/ of IE */ner/-, and the Gk. prothetic vowel has no bearing on the question of IE initial */a/.

2) Cases in which Eur. /a/ corresponds to I-I Ø initially cause no difficulty for those who believe in an IE ablaut /a/ ~ Ø, whether they express the alternation in this way or as /H_2e/- ~ /H_2/- > Ø. Nor does this alternation cause difficulty for my position because the rule expressed

above holds that initial /a/ remains in Indo-Iranian only when accented: we need merely suppose that unaccented /a/ > Ø. Nonetheless these equations, all absolutely certain, do cause trouble for Pedersen's position and are important enough to warrant separate treatment.

'dawn'	Skt. *uṣā́h,* Ave. *ušā̊,* Gk. ἠώς < **ausōs,* Lat. *aurora,* Lith. *aušrà* (M. I.113, F. I.605–606, W-H I.86).
'grow'	Skt. *úkṣati,* Ave. *uḫšye^{i}ti,* Gk. αὔξω Lat. *augeo,* Lith. *áugti* (M. I.98, F. I.187–188, W-H I.82–83).
'ear'	Ave. *uši* 'both ears', Lat. *auris* (P. 785, F. II.448–449, W-H I.85–86).
'voice'	Skt. *uditáḥ,* Gk. αὐδή (M. I.104, F. I.184).
'and/or'	Skt. *utá,* Ave. *uta,* Lat. *aut* (M. I.101, W-H I.87).

There are other examples, but these suffice to show the relation Eur. /a/ = I-I Ø, at least before /u/, and they also provide the conditioning for this relation.

There are also inner-Skt. examples which buttress the conclusion that unaccented /a/ > Ø before /u/:

ójaḥ 'strength': *ugráḥ* 'powerful' (comparative *ójīyas-*) to *ukṣ* 'grows' and cognate with Lat. *augustus* 'venerable' (M. I.131, 98–99; W-H I.82–83).

ávati 'is pleased': *unóti* 'encourages', cognate with Lat. *aveo* 'desire' (M. I.57, 104; W-H I.81).

ótum infinitive: *utáḥ* past participle of *váyati* 'weaves' cognate with Lith. *at-audaĩ* 'Einschlag' *áusti* 'weave' (M. I.132, III.147).

All show that IE */au/- remains in Indo-Iranian when accented, but loses the */a/- when unaccented. And a check of Mayrhofer's pages (M. I.130–133) shows that in fact there are no cases of unaccented initial /o/ equatable directly with IE forms containing */au/. We may therefore account for correspondences like *aurora*: *uṣā́ḥ* most economically by assuming a peculiarly I-I sound law in accordance with which IE */a/- > I-I ∅ in initial position before /u/.

The same accentual relation exists within Sanskrit also with the vowels /e/ and /i/, save that certain deictic words (*etát* 'this', *evá* 'so, exactly', *eṣá* 'this') have unaccented /e/. But these must be secondary forms, a strengthened form of /i/ in the case of *evá; tat,* and *sa* prefixed by /e/ (<*ei) in the case of *etát* and *eṣá* (M. I.127, 128). All other cases of initial /e/ in Sanskrit which are equatable with IE forms have the accent (M. I.126–130). The following equations are relevant here, though *énaḥ* may not belong (see above I.26):

édhaḥ 'fuel', Gk. *αἶθος* 'fire': *inddhé* 'sets on fire' (M. I.128, 88, F. I.37–38).

énaḥ 'crime', Gk. *αἴνυμαι* 'take': *inóti* 'advances upon' (M. I.128, 87; F. I.41).

éṣati 'seeks', Arm. *aiç* 'enquête': *iccháti* 'seeks for' (M. I.130, 85).

And the same relation Eur. */ai/- = Skt. /i/-, but without an accented Skt. /e/-, is seen in:

Gk. *αἴδομαι* 'be ashamed': Skt. *ī́ṭṭe* 'venerates' <**izdtai* (M. I.95, F. I.34–35).

We may therefore extend the rule: IE */*a*/- > ∅ /__/u/ in Indo-Iranian to include /i/ as well. And since we have found no cases of unaccented initial /a/ in Indo-Iranian, it is legitimate to present the rule governing IE */a/- as: /á/- > /á/-, but /a/ > ∅.[12]

II. In the interior of the word things are more difficult, for to Eur. /a/ (or /o/ < */a/) corresponds both /a/ (Skt. *haṁsáḥ*, Lat. *anser* 'goose') and /i/ (Skt. *sthitáḥ*, Lat. *status*, past participle of *stā-* 'stand'). Furthermore, though the /a/ = /i/ equation is well established by many secure etymologies, the /a/ = /a/ equation is frequently most problematic. Scholars will differ as to what cognates they will admit as evidence for IE /a/ (Eur. /a/ = I-I /a/), but the following list at least will likely be accepted by all, regardless of how they choose to symbolize the reconstructed segment:

1. Skt. *haṁsáḥ* 'goose', Gk. χήν 'id.', Lat. *anser* 'id.' < **ghans* (U. 356, B. 1058, W-H I.52, Szemerényi 1964:8).
2. Skt. *nas-* 'nose', OCS *nosъ* OHG *nasa*, Lat. *nāsus*, *nāres* < **nas-* (M. II.146, W-H II.143–144, Pedersen 1900:82, Szemerényi 1964:8).
3. Skt. *devár-* 'brother of husband', Gk. δαήρ, Lat. *levir* < **daiwér-* (M. II.65, F. I.338–339, W-H I.787–788, Kuryłowicz 1956:191, Szemerényi 1964:8).
4. Skt. *bhájati* 'deal out', Gk. ἔφαγον 'eat' < **bhag-* (M. II.463–464, B. 1010, Wackernagel 1896:78, Pedersen 1900:82, Kuryłowicz 1956:191).
5. Skt. *grásati* 'swallow, devour', Gk. γράω 'gnaw, eat' < **gras-* (M. I.352, F. I.326, Wackernagel 1896:78, Pedersen 1900:82).
6. Skt. *héṣaḥ* 'arrow', Gk. χαῖος 'shepherd's staff' <**ghais-* (U. 362, B. 1046, Kuryłowicz 1956:192).
7. Skt. *tvak* 'skin', Gk. σάκος 'shield' <**twak* (M. I.537, B. 849, Kuryłowicz 1956:190).

All these examples contain /a/ in the initial syllable of the word, and that /a/ is either accented (4–7); or appears in a monosyllable (1–2; **ghans* must have been the IE word for 'goose', and the Skt. and Lat. forms later extensions of it); or in a syllable closed with /y/ (3), from which we may generalize to: a syllable closed by a resonant.

Given the above environmental specifications we can then admit the following as evidence for IE */a/:

8. Skt. *daṁsaḥ* 'marvelous power', Gk. δήνεα 'counsels, plans, arts' < **dansos* (M. II.9, F. I.382, Pedersen 1900:78).

9. Skt. *dáśati* 'bites', Gk. δακεῖν 'id.' < **dak-* (M. II.27, F. I.343–344). But it may be that the /a/ in both the Gk. and the Skt. forms derives from */n/.

10. Skt. *dáyate* 'divides, imparts', Gk. δαίομαι 'divide, distribute' < **day-* (M. II.20–21, F. I.341–342). Cf. also Skt. PPP. *dináḥ, ditáḥ* and Gk. δατέομαι 'divide among themselves'.

11. Skt. *dháyati* 'sucks, drinks', Goth. *daddjan* 'suck', OCS *dojǫ* 'suck'< **dhay-* (M. II.93, Hübschmann 1885:79). But the vowel in these cases may have been */o/ as expected in causative formations (Burrow 1949:43, Kuryłowicz 1956:166).

12. *śatsyati* 'fall (fut.)', Lat. *cado* 'fall' < **kad-* (P. 516, E-M 82, Kuryłowicz 1956:191).

13. Skt. *kadanam* 'destruction', Gk. κεκαδών 'deprive of' < **kad-* (M. I.149, F. I.811).

14. Skt. *śāśáda* 'excel', Gk. κέκαδμαι 'excel' < **kad-* (P. 516–517, F. I.811–812, Pedersen 1900:82). Kuryłowicz (1956:192) holds that the attested forms of *śad-* do not exclude a root with long vowel (*śād-*).

15. Skt. *kekaraḥ* 'squint-eyed', Lat. *caecus* 'blind', Goth. *haihs* 'one-eyed' < **kaiko-* (W-H I.129, Kuryłowicz 1956:190). Mayrhofer (I.264) feels that this relation is in no way certain because of the late attestation of *kekaraḥ*, the by-forms not exampled in literature (*kedaraḥ*, *terakaḥ*), and because European cognates come only from the western European area. Szemerényi (1964:8) regards this as one of the surest examples of IE */a/.

16. Skt. *kéśaram* 'hair', Lat. *caesaries* 'the hair' < **kais-* (M. I.268, W-H I.133, though there are phonological difficulties signaled by Kuryłowicz 1956:193).

17. Skt. *kévaṭa* 'cave, hollow', Gk. καίατα·ὀρύγματα Hes. <**kaiw-* (F. I.753, Kuryłowicz 1956:190; Mayrhofer I.267 feels that the connection of these words is unlikely).

18. Skt. *kevalaḥ* 'exclusively one's own', Lat. *caelebs* 'unmarried' <**kail-* (M. I.267, W-H I.130).

19. Skt. *kalyaḥ* 'healthy', Gk. καλλίων 'fairer' <**kaly-* (M. I.184–185, F. I.767, Pedersen 1900:77).

20. Skt. *śamnīte* 'toils', Gk. κάμνω 'work' <**ḱam-* (F. I.773–774, Cardona 1960:502–507). It is perhaps more usual to derive these forms from */km/-.

21. Skt. *kanīnaḥ* 'young', *kánīyān* 'younger', Gk. καινός 'new' <**kany-* (M. I.151, F. I.754).

22. Skt. *śaṅkú-* 'peg', Welsh *cainc* 'branch', ON *hár* 'Ruderklamp', OCS *sok* 'branch' <**ḱanku-* (P. 523, Kuryłowicz 1956:191, Szemerényi 1964:8).

23. Skt. *karkaṭaḥ* 'crab', Gk. καρκίνος 'crab', Lat. *cancer* 'id.' (<**karkaros* by dissimilation) <**kar-* (M.

I.169, F. I.789–790, W-H I.151, Pedersen 1900:77, Kuryłowicz 1956:190, 193).

24. Skt. _karkaraḥ_ 'hard, firm', Gk. κάρκαρος·τραχύς Hes. <*_karkar-_ (F. I.789; M. I.170 is dubious). Kuryłowicz (1956:192) says the form rests on intensive reduplication, and Burrow (1945:97–98) feels that the Skt. word is connected with _kharaḥ_ 'hard, rough, sharp', and that both are of Dravidian origin.

25. Skt. _mádati_ 'rejoice, be intoxicated', Gk. μαδάω 'be moist', Lat. _madeo_ 'be wet, be drunk' <*_mad-_ (F. II.157–158, Wackernagel 1896:78, Pedersen 1900:83; E-M 377 exclude comparison with the Skt. form, and Kuryłowicz (1956:189) denies that the Skt. form derives from *_mad-_ because of Gk. μεστος which points to an */e/ vowel).

26. Skt. _paṅkaḥ_ 'mud, mire', Gaul. _ana_ 'palus', MIr. _an_ 'eau', Goth. _fani_ 'Schlamm' <*_pan-_ (M. II.184, Kuryłowicz 1956:191).

27. Skt. _rábhate_ 'ergreift', Gk. λάφυρα 'booty' <*_labh-_ (M. III.42–43, F. II.91, Pedersen 1900:83).

28. Skt. _rábhaḥ_ 'violence, impetuosity', Lat. _rabies_ 'rage, madness' <*_rabh-_ (M. III.43, W-H II.413, E-M 562, Pedersen 1900:82).

29. Skt. _skándati_ 'springs', Lat. _scando_ 'climb', Gk. σκάνδαλον 'trap' <*_skand-_ (B. 870, E-M 599, W-H II.488, Wackernagel 1896:78, Pedersen 1900:78).

30. Skt. _svádati_ 'taste well to', Gk. ἁνδάνω 'please' <*_swad-_ (F. I.104, Pedersen 1900:77; Hübschmann 1885:59–60 feels that *_swad-_ < *_swnd-_, but this seems unlikely).

31. Skt. _tavīti_ 'être fort, avoir la puissance, pouvoir', Gk.

ταῦς·μέγας, ταῦσας·μεγαλύνας, πλεονάσας Hes. <**taw-* (B. 945–946, Kuryłowicz 1956:190; M. I.490, though he accepts the equation, finds difficulties with it).

32. Skt. *váñcati* 'totter, stagger', Lat. *vacillare* 'sway to and fro' <**wak-* (W-H I.268, M. III.127 hesitantly; E-M 710 regard *vacillare* as an expressive word of obscure origin; Kuryłowicz 1956:189 feels that these forms cannot be related because of the complete absence of the nasal in the Lat. word).

33. Skt. *vastu* 'place, thing', Gk. (F)ἄστυ 'town' <**wastu* U. 279, F. I.173–174, Kuryłowicz 1956:191).

34. Skt. *yájati* 'worships, sacrifices', Gk. ἅζομαι 'stand in awe of' <**yag-* (M. III.3–4, Pedersen 1900:77; F. I.10 feels that the Gk. word is 'nicht sicher erklärt' and hence not certainly to be compared with Skt. *yájati;* E-M 587 favor connection of Gk. ἅγιος with Lat. *sacer*).

All of the above are positive instances of a rule:

$$/a/ > /a/ \quad / \left[\begin{array}{l} \_\_\,'C \\ \_\_\,RC \end{array}\right]$$

but there are several counterexamples not accounted for by the rule, words which contain unaccented /a/ in an open syllable: Skt. *śaṇáḥ* 'a kind of hemp', *vaśā́* 'cow, barren cow', *śaśáḥ* 'hare'.

Skt. *śaṇáḥ,* Gk. κάνναβις (Lat. *cannabis*) OE *hænep,* OCS *konoplja* are clearly related (U. 301–302, F. I.779, W-H I.154, Kuryłowicz 1956:191), but are just as clearly all loans from some non-IE source. This conclusion is indicated both by the nature of the thing designated, as well as by (1) the Slavic /k/ which excludes direct connection with Skt. *śaṇáḥ,* and by (2) the Skt. cerebral /ṇ/. Furthermore the word is not restricted to Indo-European, for the Sumerian *kunibu* must also be related. Hence this word is not a true counterexample because it was not in the language at the time that unaccented /a/ was passing to [ə].

Skt. *vaśā́,* Lat. *vacca* (U. 278, W-H II.722, Pedersen 1900:77, Kuryłowicz 1956:191) is more difficult, for the lack of exact identity in the velars is not sufficient to cause one to discard the equation. But there are various reasons for doubting that the words are related. In the first place the word occurs in only two IE languages, languages which share vocabulary generally only in the religious and legal spheres (Palmer 1961:25), and not in the agricultural. Second, the meanings diverge: the Skt. word seems to mean primarily 'barren', and can be used both of cows and women, while the Lat. word does seem primarily to mean 'cow'. Third, if the words are cognate, and if the original meaning was 'cow', then the IE word denoted only the female of a domestic animal, a distinction according to sex not made with most other domestic animals (E-M 710). And finally there are other words within Sanskrit with which *vaśā́* might better be compared: either *vā́śati* 'heult, blökt', or *ukṣā́* 'bull' (U. 278), and certainly *vāśitā́* 'rindernde Kuh' (Wackernagel 1896:226); and in Latin we might connect *vacca* with *vaccinium* 'blueberry' on the assumption that they are related Mediterranean words, though *vaccinium* is usually connected rather with Gk. *ὑάκινθος* 'hyacinth' (W-H II.722). None of these considerations taken alone or together would be sufficient to destroy the connection, but they are sufficient when the word also goes against a rule (if unaccented */a/ > I-I */i/ be accepted as a rule) of IE phonology.[13]

Skt. *śaśáḥ* 'hare', Lat. *cānus* (<**casnos*) 'gray, white', Osc. *casnar* 'old', Welsh *ceinach* (<**kasnī*) 'hare', OHG *haso,*

OPruss. *sasins* (U. 306, F. I.812, W-H I.156, Kuryłowicz 1956:191). Though this equation has been considered certain by many (Szemerényi 1964:8), and indeed appears solid, it is in reality not so. In the first place the Skt. form requires that we assume an assimilation of *ś—s* to *ś—ś*, an assimilation nowhere else attested (Mayrhofer 1952:29), and further that we posit a thematic derivation of **ḱas-*, a derivative not to be found in any other language. This equation also leaves completely unexplained the Gk. form κεκῆνας·λαγωούς.κρῆτες (Hes.), a form which one would ordinarily compare with the Sanskrit, deriving both from **ḱeḱ-* (or possibly *ḱeḱes-*). Mayrhofer (1952) in fact does just this, and in turn connects these words with *śaśati* 'springs' (<**ḱeḱeti*). He further assumes that **kas-* 'white, gray' is a European word only, an assumption shared by Ernout-Meillet (94). An IE ***ḱasós* should have developed to Skt. **śisáḥ*, not *śaśáḥ*.[14]

If */a/ occurs only in closed syllables or accented, schwa must occur only elsewhere: the following cognates show under what conditions [ə] appears:[15]

35. Skt. *damitáḥ* 'tamed', Gk. ἀδάματος 'unconquered', Lat. *domitor* 'tamer' <**domat-* (M. II.19, F. I.346, W-H I.367–368).

36. Skt. *duhitā́*, Gk. θυγάτηρ, Goth. *daúhtar* 'daughter' <**dhugatér* (M. II.56, F. I.690).

37. Skt. *śamitár-* 'preparer, dresser', Gk. κάματος 'toil, trouble' <**ḱamat-* (U. 303, 308; F. I.773).

38. The *-ni-* of Skt. ninth-class verbs (e.g. *mṛṇimáḥ* 'crush' beside *mṛṇā́mi*) and the -να- of Gk. verbs like δάμναμεν 'subdue' beside δάμνᾱμι (de Saussure 1922:224).

39. Skt. *pitár-*, Gk. πατήρ, Lat. *pater* 'father' <**patér*.

40. Skt. *sthitáḥ* 'standing', Gk. στατός 'placed', Lat. *status* 'set, fixed' <**statós* (U. 347, F. I.739, W-H II.596–599).

41. Skt. *śiṣṭáḥ* 'taught', Lat. *castus* 'morally pure' <**ḱastós* (U. 308–309, E-M 104; W-H I.179–180 deny any connection between these words).

Thus schwa occurs only unaccented, whether in initial or noninitial syllables, and in initial syllables only before a single consonant /t/, or before /st/, a cluster which may well not have closed a preceding syllable in Indo-European. There is therefore no contrast between [a] and [ə] in any environment, and hence no reason to distinguish them phonemically. We need only the rule: IE unaccented */a/ passes to [ə] (I-I /i/) in syllables not closed by a resonant.

Further cognates, some of them questionable, support the rule just given:

42. Skt. *iṣiráḥ* 'refreshing, fresh; flourishing, vigorous', Gk. ἱαρός, ἱερός 'holy' <**isarós* (M. I.93, F. I.712–714).

43. Skt. *madiráḥ* 'intoxicating', Gk. μαδαρός 'wet' <**madarós* (M. II.569, F. II.157–158).

44. Skt. *párīman-* 'plentifully', Gk. πέλανος 'thick liquid substance' <**péla-* (M. II.219, F. II.494).

45. Skt. *prathimā́* 'extension, width', Gk. πλαταμών 'broad flat body' <**plata-* (M. II.364, F. II.554).

46. Skt. *támisrā* 'a dark night', Lat. *tenebrae* 'darkness' <**témas-* (M. I.479, W-H II.664).

47. Skt. *śitáḥ* 'sharpened' (PPP of *śā-*), Lat. *catus* 'sharp, shrill' <**ḱatós* (U. 311, W-H I.183–184).

48. Skt. *śárītoḥ* 'crushed' (PPP of *śṛ-*), Gk. κεραΐζω 'ravage, plunder' <**ḱéra-* (U. 315, F. I.822).

49. Skt. *chitáḥ* 'cut up' (PPP of *chā-*), Gk. *σχάω* 'slit open' <**ska-* (M. I.410, B. 931–932, W-H II. 495–496; Burrow 1949:47 analyzes the root as **skeH-*, **skHi-*).

50. Skt. *vámiti* 'vomits', Gk. *ἐμέω* (if from **ἐμάω*) 'id.', Lat. *vomitus* 'id.' <*(*w*)*éma-* (M. III.146, F. I.505, W-H II.835).

Just as there were apparent instances of unaccented /a/ in an open syllable, there are also cases of accented Skt. /i/ which would seem at first sight to cast doubt on the distributional statement just made, and which must be disposed of before we can accept my rule. The first group of exceptions, cited by Güntert (1916:13–14) and Brugmann (1897:173), is composed of cases of accented /i/ deriving from schwa in the initial syllable, a position in which we would expect /a/. Such cases are: *sthítiḥ* 'standing' from *sthā-* 'stand'; *dítiḥ* 'generosity, distributing' from *dā-* 'give'; *sídhyati* 'succeed' beside *sādh-* 'reach one's goal'. Unfortunately Güntert wrote at a time when the philological investigation of Sanskrit had not yet reached a very advanced level, and hence relied on forms not sufficient to support his arguments. To take the forms in reverse order: Renou (1964:164–165) has recently called into question the connection of the late Vedic hapax *sídhyati* with the root *sādh-*. And even if the roots are related, they cannot be used as evidence for accented schwa, for the words are Indo-Iranian only, not Indo-European. And one of the requirements for establishing IE schwa for a morpheme is that it both contain Skt. /i/ and show /a/ in a European language. Mayrhofer (M. 439–440) doubts that there ever existed in Sanskrit a form *dítiḥ* beside the regular *dā́ti* and -°*tti*; Güntert thus was using a vox nihili. *sthítiḥ,* though a real form, is not exampled until the *Śatapatha Brahmaṇa,* a period in which the accent of many such forms was being drawn back from the ending to the stem (Wackernagel 1954:622ff., esp. 631), thus allowing for the possibility at least that in early Vedic times *sthī́tiḥ* was in fact oxytone. But in any event abstracts in *-ti-*, regardless of the attested place of the accent, were formed with the reduced grade of the root (Wackernagel 1954:629) and the reduced grade appears only unaccented. Too, analogy with *sthitáḥ*, invoked by Pedersen (1900:84) is not impossible. These examples do not invalidate the rule.

The other part of Güntert's argument (1916:13–14) concerns nouns in *-tra-* (Wackernagel 1954:701ff.) like (51) *arítra-* 'oar' which is usually compared with Gk. ἐρέτης 'oarsman', but is in fact more likely to be related to Gk. ἐλατήρ 'driver' (Bechtel 1892:205), both deriving from something that could be written in traditional orthography as **erə-t-* (or **elə-t-*). Instances of this sort do constitute an exception to Pedersen's rule, at least at first blush, but do not as yet constitute an exception to my formulation, since I have assigned a role to the accent only in initial syllables: it is possible that, accented or not, all */a/ in interior syllables passed to [ə] and thence to /i/ in Indo-Iranian. Such an assumption would be phonologically acceptable, but the cases in question do not favor this conclusion. Similar formations in Greek, such as τέρετρον 'borer, gimlet' and ἄροτρον 'plow' are accented on the initial syllable, not on the schwa, and many scholars in order to posit a single protoform have assumed a secondary accent shift to the second syllable well within the history of Sanskrit (Hirt 1900:7, Kuryłowicz 1958:68). And Pedersen (1900:84), without positing an accent shift, invokes the influence of the agent noun *aritár-* 'rower'. Thus it seems that these cases neither constitute an exception to Pedersen's rule nor favor a rule: */a/ (regardless of accent) > [ə] > /i/ in interior syllables in Indo-Iranian.

Much the same can be said also of the pair:

52. Skt. *kravíḥ,* 'raw flesh', Gk. *κρέας* 'meat' (<**krewəs* F. II.12, M. I.277, W-H I.294–295).

The words differ in the place of the accent, and it is again perhaps indicated to assume that the Skt. accent has shifted from the stem to the ending after *rocíḥ* 'light', *śocíḥ* 'flame', etc., and that Greek has preserved the original place of accent. This seems a better solution than assuming the opposite, and there is therefore no need to deny connection between these words as is done by Pedersen (1900: 77—*kravíḥ* < **krewis*) and Burrow (1949:54—*kravíḥ* < **kreuHis, κρέας* < **kreuHos*). Both the Gk. and the Skt. forms derive from **kréwas.*

Neither of the above comparisons speaks in favor of assuming that all IE */a/, accented or not, pass to /i/ in noninitial syllables. What is more, two forms urge that we retain Pedersen's formulation and assign a role to the accent in internal syllables as well as initially:

53. Skt. *jaráḥ* (V) 'old age', Gk. *γέρας* 'prize', *γῆρας* 'old age' (M. I.421, F. I.299).

54. *-*kás* in Skt. *parvaśáḥ* 'gliedweise', Gk. *ἀνδρακάς* 'man by man' (Wackernagel 1888:144, Schwyzer 1939:630, F. I.473).

In the first case there is no doubt that the forms are related, but there is doubt as to the original shape of the word. Both Frisk and Mayrhofer seem to assume an original **gerós* (<**gerəos* ??) as the ancestor of the Skt. form, an assumption for which I can see no need or justification, though of course there is no argument sufficient to refute it. Rather it seems that the Gk. form has once again preserved the original accent (though we could perhaps just as easily assume the opposite) and that the ancestor form was IE **géras*. But in this case apparently the shift of the accent in Indo-Iranian from first syllable to stem vowel took place early, before the phonetic change of unaccented /a/ to [ə]. The regular development of unaccented */a/ is seen in *jarimā́* 'decrepitude, old age' (M. I.422).

The second case seems to allow for no doubt whatsoever. Schwyzer (1939:630) compares Gk. ἑκάς 'afar off' and ἀνδρακάς 'man by man' with Skt. *dviśáḥ* 'zu zweien, paarweise' and *gaṇaśáḥ* 'in Scharen'; Frisk (I.473) compares the Gk. words with Skt. *śataśáḥ* 'hundert für hundert, zu Hunderten'; and Wackernagel (1888:144) followed by Pedersen (1900:82) compared *parvaśáḥ* 'gliedweise' d.i. 'mit Sonderung der Glieder'. There seems to be general agreement that the forms are related, and since they are accented on the same syllable, we must reconstruct an IE suffix *-*ḱás*, and must assume further that it was the accent which prevented the change of I-I */a/ to [ə] to /i/. Hence the rule for internal syllables will be the same as that for initial syllables: unaccented IE */a/ passes to I-I /i/ in open syllables.

The above lists and discussions do not produce the 250 cognates Kuryłowicz (1956:189) feels reasonably to be expected from the number of initial correspondences. But there are a number of reasons which can be alleged to account for this discrepancy, a discrepancy which in any event is created by Kuryłowicz's expectations and is far from inevitable (Szemerényi 1964:9). In the first place there is the role played by historical accident: a number of words attested only in European languages may well once have existed in Indo-Iranian but have been dropped because of the strikingly different cultural milieu into which the I-I peoples moved. Examples of this possibility include (list from Szemerényi 1964:9; a longer list in Kuryłowicz 1956:194–195):

IE **bhardhā* 'beard': Lat. *barba,* OHG *bart,*
OCS *brada* (Russ. *boroda*)
IE **laiwo-* 'left': Gk. *λαιός*, Lat. *laevus,* OCS *lěvъ*
IE **skaiwo-* 'left': Gk. *σκαιός*, Lat. *scaevus*

And furthermore, roots containing */a/, if of a morphological category generally displaying ablaut, may well have been remodeled to /e/ ~ /o/ on the analogy of the at the time most prevalent type (Szemerényi 1964:9). Such may yet be visible in roots which seem to show an */a/ ~ */e/ variation, roots like: **ḱas-* ~ **ḱes* 'cut' (Appendix II *27) *(s)*kand-* ~ *(s)*kend-* 'brilliant (vel sim.)' (Appendix II *21), **kratos* ~ **kretos* 'power' (Appendix II *30). Thus we find that the number of instances of */a/ in interior syllables is greater than had been supposed, and we have some reason to believe that it may in fact have been greater still.

III. In final position there are relatively few cognate pairs bearing on the question of */a/ and schwa, but there is no question about what cases are to be considered. They include:

a) Skt. *véda* 'I know', Gk. *οἶδα* 'id.'
Skt. *véttha* 'you (sg.) know', Gk. *οἶσθα* 'id.'

both of which show an /a/ = /a/ correspondence, and:

b) Skt. *ábharāmahi* 'we were carrying (mid.), Gk. *ἐφερόμεθα* 'id.'
Skt. *bháranti* 'carrying (ntr. plur.)', Gk. *φέροντα* 'id.'
Skt. *máhi* 'big (ntr. sg.)', Gk. *μέγα* 'id.'

all of which show an /a/ = /i/ correspondence, the correspondence usually subsumed under schwa. The two phonemic solutions for these contrasts most generally entertained clearly differentiate these correspondences by using different symbols:

	a	*b*
laryngeal	/H_2e/	/H/
traditional	/a/	/ə/

The traditional solution, though, has been weakened by our having shown above that [ə] elsewhere in the word is merely the unaccented allophone of /a/: it would be strange indeed if Indo-European had a phoneme /ə/ differentiated from /a/ only in final position and only in three words or grammatical categories. Hence the traditional solution must be given up. The laryngeal solution suffers from this same weakness, for only finally would /H_2e/ contrast with /H/; but not to the same extent, for /H/ is supposed to occur after consonants elsewhere (as in **stHtós*), and also before pause (as in **pótniH*). But this may be the only case of -CH#, and this fact would tend to weaken the laryngealist position.

Other scholars, however, have declined to reconstruct two entities for this position in the word, and have supposed that all those Gk. and Skt. forms containing /a/ derive from IE */a/, while Skt. forms containing /i/ continue original IE (or I-I) */i/. This position of course involves denying that the final segments of the cognates listed above in b) are related. In order to decide the question whether [ə] = /a/ in final position, we shall have to discuss the relevant cases individually, perhaps best beginning with /a/ = /i/.

1. Skt. *ábharāmahi* = Gk. *ἐφερόμεϑα*. Pedersen (1900: 80–81) pointed out that the functional identity of the endings of these words is only a postulate, since the Gk. form is both primary and secondary, the Skt. form secondary only: Gk. *-μεϑα* could just as easily be compared with *-mahe,* the primary ending. Furthermore the inner-Skt. relation: 2d sg. mid. *bhárase,* 2d sg. act. *bhárasi* is parallel

to that seen in *-mahe*, *-mahi*. And perhaps most important, it is by no means certain that Indo-European possessed a primary:secondary distinction in the first person plural middle, and it is therefore possible that the Indic distinction is an innovation. He concludes that it would not be unreasonable to assume that *-mahe* and *-μεϑα* were phonologically distinct forms of the same original morpheme, and that *-mahi* (cf. 1st sg. *júhve*: *ájuhvi* 'sacrifice') is just as much an innovation as the subjunctive ending *-mahai*. Burrow (1949:57), remarking simply on the series *-mahi*: *-mahe*: *-mahai*, concludes that the /i/ is an original /i/. And Hirt (1928:149) separates the forms by regarding *-μεϑα* as *-me-* plus the particle *-dha*, *-mahi* as *-me-* plus the particle *-dhi*.

Güntert (1916:12) objects to Pedersen's separating the two forms on the very good grounds that they are so clearly related that really impressive arguments are needed to separate them: and Pedersen's arguments are not really impressive. Güntert willingly concedes that Sanskrit has innovated in introducing a primary : secondary distinction in this category, but feels that the innovation concerns *-mahe*, not *-mahi*. And it does seem that this is the most reasonable solution. For if we assume that the original ending was -**medha*, we can then account for the Skt. situation quite simply by assuming that *-i* was optionally added in the primary tenses (cf. Vedic *-masi* beside *-maḥ* in the 1st plural active) after the analogy of other primary middle endings (*-ai*, *-sai*, *-tai*; *-ntai*), a development which resulted in:

primary	*secondary*
{ *-medha* / *-medhai* }	*-medha*

with *-medha* and *-medhai* in more or less free variation in primary tenses. Later final -/a/ passed to -/i/, and the shorter form became *-mahi*, thus giving the forms:

primary	*secondary*
{*-mahi*, *-mahe*}	*-mahi*

At this point the opposition between *-mahe* and *-mahi* was grammaticalized, and *-mahe*, originally an optional variant, took over alone as the primary form, *-mahi* as the secondary. Thus a primary : secondary distinction arose in the first person of the plural as well as elsewhere. Such seems the simplest solution, but is of course predicated on the assumption that final I-I *-/a/ > -/i/. But it is already interesting and important that the simplest solution points to this conclusion, a conclusion quite in keeping with our assumptions about unaccented */a/ in other positions in the word.

2. *bhắranti* = *φέροντα*. This equation, though accepted for many years, has also been questioned for many years, first by Schmidt (1889:227ff.), then by Pedersen (1900: 79–80), and most recently by Burrow (1949:46), all of whom assume that the final -/i/ in Sanskrit is an original IE */i/ and not */a/ or */ə/. The reason for this, at first sight, strange conclusion seems to be that the Skt. -/i/ is not obligatory in the Veda, and does not seem to be the most ancient form of the neuter plural, hence presumably not of IE date. And since not of IE date, not IE */a/, but I-I */i/, which is then assumed to have derived, not from IE */a/, but from IE */i/.

And indeed there is good reason to believe that in Indo-European the neuter plural was not well established as a morphological category. Leaving aside the vowel stems, we find that Vedic has the following neuter plural forms (data from Lanman 1880):

stem	*short form*	*long form*
-n	ahā, śīrṣā	ahāni, śīrṣāṇi (Lanman 538–539)
-nt	———	sānti (Lanman 510)
-s	———	-āṅsi (Lanman 566)

Other stem forms are not represented in the Veda. What is common to all these forms is the length of the stem-final vowel, a mark common also to vocalic stems when inflected for the plural, and what is common to the longer forms alone is the nasal and the /i/. It is therefore possible to state that there are two types of neuter plural, both of which involve lengthening of the stem-final vowel, and that the second involves also the addition of -/ni/ to the stem-vowel thus lengthened:

1) lengthen stem-final vowel
2) (optional) add -/ni/ to stem-final vowel

But these rules cause trouble, slight though it be, with *sānti,* which would come out by these rules as: 1) **sānt,* 2) **sānint,* forms which would in turn become **sān* (and possibly **sā*) and **sānin,* respectively, because of the rules of sentence sandhi. It seems, then, that this formulation is incorrect and must be replaced. Since final -/n/ disappears in sentence sandhi after a long vowel, it seems most economical to state the first (obligatory) rule for the formation of Skt. neuter plurals as:

1) add /:n/ to stem-final vowel

The effect of this rule would clearly be nullified by the sandhi rules, and in fact produces the shorter forms *ahā* and *śīrṣā* above: **sānt* would appear again as **sān* (or **sā*), *-āns* would appear as *-ās* (generally). The operation of this sandhi rule was, however, prevented by (optional) rule 2) which preserved the morphological identity of these forms:

2) (optional) add /i/ to final consonant

This -/i/ was optional in Vedic Skt., was an Indic -/i/, and nothing can as yet be stated about its origin.

A similar situation obtains in Avestan Persian, save that here short forms are better represented (Bartholomae 1895:132–133, Brugmann 1911:235–237):

stem	*short form*	*long form*
-n	dāmąn	afšmānī
-r	ayār^{ə}	———
-s	sravå	var^{ə}čāhī
-nt	mīždavąn	———

The only difference between this situation and the Vedic involves the nasal, and the rules:

1) lengthen stem-final vowel
2) (optional) add /i/ to final consonant

will handle all these forms. The nasal is not present in Avestan, and can easily be explained as secondary in Indic. We may therefore regard the Avestan rules as essentially the I-I rules, confirmation for which comes from the nasalless Indic *catvāri* 'four'.

The fact that the addition of -/i/ is an optional rule even in Indo-Iranian does not of itself prove that -/i/ derives from something other than IE */a/ (= [ə]). But there is evidence supporting such a conclusion. Burrow (1949:46), followed by Palmer (1961:246), feels that the case for */i/ is clinched by the situation in Hittite. For Hittite, it is clear, beside cases of I-I rule 1) (which must now be taken as IE rule 1) such as *kurur*$^{\text{ḪI.A}}$ 'enemies', also has forms which seem to conform to rule 2), such as *kururi*$^{\text{ḪI.A}}$, thus suggesting that rule 2) also is of IE date. If one identifies the I-I /i/ with this Hittite /i/, then clearly *φέροντα* and *bharanti* are no longer directly comparable, but are different adaptations of something that may have been **bherōnt*. That is: rule 1) will have applied everywhere, but Greek will have rewritten rule 2), now obligatory, to: add /a/. The reasons for the Gk. substitution of /a/ for /i/ will remain unelucidated by this theory.

But the Hittite evidence is in fact not conclusive, for Hittite also has neuter plurals in *-a*, and it is therefore not justifiable to compare I-I -/i/ solely with Hitt. *-i*. One must take into account also Hitt. *-a*, the more so because *i*-forms are restricted to a) *i*-stems and b) *-r*, *-l*, and *-r/-n* stems, and do not occur (save for *ḫumanti* 'all') in *-nt-* stems. In *-r*, *-l*, and *-r/-n* stems they alternate with no ending at all, while in *i*-stems they alternate with *-a*. Brosman (1962: 63–65) has suggested that the *-i* in *i*-stems is the original stem of the word without any ending, and that the *-a* of *i*-stems, occurring mostly in adjectives, represents a contraction of *-aḭa*, an ending which also occurs. In the liquid stems *-i* replaces Ø, and hence provides a means of distinguishing the singular from the plural in these stems. The reason that *-a*, the ending of other consonant stems, was not chosen for this function is that in the *i*-stems a distinction had arisen between *-i*, which occurred mostly in nouns, and *-a* < *-aḭa*, which occurred mostly in adjectives. And since *-r*, *-l*, *-r/-n* words were mostly nouns, *-i* was extended to them; and conversely, since *-nt-* stems were mostly adjectives, the *-i* ending made no inroads on the original *-a*. Hence the *-i* is a secondary entry into the neuter plural, not an inherited ending, and not to be compared phonologically with I-I -/i/. On Brosman's interpretation, therefore, Hittite also had an -/a/ in neuter plurals, and Hitt. -/i/ does not provide support for interpreting I-I -/i/ as IE */i/. We should compare *bharanti* = φέροντα = *ḫumanta,* deriving all from original *-*ōnta.*[16]

3. Skt. *mahi* = Gk. μέγα. This comparison, which has frequently been made, and which provides one of the cornerstones for the doctrine of final -/ə/, is the weakest of

those thus far discussed. Evidence for -/a/, aside from the Gk. form, is provided by Arm. *mec* 'gross', instr. *mecaw;* and for -/i/, aside from the Skt. form, by Goth. *mikils* 'gross' (<PGmc. **mekilaz:* Szemerényi 1952:48–49) and Hitt. *mekki* 'sehr', *mekkis* 'gross'. There can be no doubt that these words are related, but there is doubt as to the quality of the second vowel.[17] It rather seems as if different language groups have adapted an uninflected **meg-* to their own inflectional tastes in various ways. In view of this uncertainty, it is perhaps best not to use this comparison as evidence for the development of final -*/a/. But at the very least *μέγα* = *mahi* does not prove incompatible with a rule which provides that final -/a/ > [ə] > I-I -/i/.

And it does in fact seem to be a rule that IE final */a/ appears as /i/ in absolute final position in Sanskrit. Another case is provided by:

4. Skt. *íti* 'so, auf diese Weise', Lat. *ita* 'thus, so' (M. I.86, E-M 325; W-H I.722–723 deny the connection).

The question then arises whether all final */a/ pass to /i/, or whether some remain -/a/, a question that is answered by the equation:

5. Skt. *ihá* 'here' (Pali *idha,* Ave. *iδa,* OP *idā*), Gk. *ἰθαγενής* 'aboriginal' (M. I.94, F. I.715). Cf. Lat. *ibi* (<**idhai*), though some take this from **idhei* (W-H I.722–723).

From this one case we can see that the same rule applies in final position as elsewhere: unaccented /a/ > /i/.

Two cases remain, however, two important cases which yield a result counter to rule and to expectation:

6. Skt. *véda* 'I know', Gk. *οἶδα* 'id.' < **woida* (P. 1125, F. II.357).

7. Skt. *véttha* 'you (sg.) know', Gk. *οἶσθα* 'id', the second person singular of **woida*, < **woitstha* (= //woidsdha//).

Neither of these words contains accented /a/, so both are exceptions to my rule.[18] Various solutions to the opposition *veda* ≠ *bharanti* have been proposed. 1) The traditional explanation again posits the two phonemes /a/ and /ə/, while 2) the laryngeal explanation, in doing in fact the same thing, derives the forms from **woidH₂e* (and **woidstH₂e*) and **bherontH* respectively. And the laryngeal hypothesis finds impressive support for **woidH₂e* in the Hitt. *-hi* conjugation frequently, though not always, compared with the IE perfect. For the endings of the first and second persons singular of this conjugation are *-ḫi* (Luvian preterite *-ḫa*) and *-ti*, with, in the first person, the /h/ demanded by the theory. And in the second person the /h/ is supposed once to have been present because the /i/ did not palatalize the /t/ to /z/, as it did for instance in /ti/ > /zi/ in the third person singular of verbs of the *-mi* conjugation. But the second part of this argument is incorrect, for *-ti* must derive from earlier **tai* (or **thai*) (Kuryłowicz 1958ᵃ: 236), and so the absence of palatalization is to be expected. But the /h/ (though not the /e/!) of the first person is assured, and it is therefore not impossible that IE */h/, once present in the IE form, prevented the passage of IE */woidha/ to Skt. */vedi/. Thus far we might be inclined to go along with the laryngealist argument, an argument originally framed in other terms. But the */h/ will have prevented the passage of */a/ (attested in Greek, Sanskrit, and Luvian) to /i/, not the passage of (unattested) */e/ to /i/, or indeed have caused the passage of */e/ to */a/. And it will have been an IE phoneme */h/, not an IE morphophoneme //H// with the properties of appearing now as [:], now as [ə], now as [h]. We shall below provide another explanation for the preservation of -/a/ in Indo-Iranian, without taking a stand on whether the IE form was **woidha* or **woida*.

3) Pedersen (1900:78–81) and Burrow (1949:45–46, 57), as we have seen, deny the connection of Skt. forms in -/i/ with European forms in -/a/, and derive /a/ = /a/ from IE */a/. But we have seen also that their denial of the correspondence -/i/ = -/a/ is unjustified. 4) Another explanation derives both Skt. reflexes from IE */a/. Thus Wackernagel (1896:6) states: 'Dunkel bleibt vorläufig, warum von den Personalendungen, welche griechischen auf *a* entsprechen, die einen *i* haben: *-mahi*, *-vahi*, die andern *a*: *-a*, *-tha* des perf.'. And Pedersen, abandoning his position of 1900, holds (1926:27): 'La fin de mot -a (-ə) a donné en sanskrit tantôt -a, tantôt -i (mahi = gr. μέγα); c'est à tort que j'ai voulu nier une des alternatives, *KZ* 36,76ss. Je crois maintenant que -a est le traitement de la pause, -i le traitement du sandhi.' What Wackernagel found inexplicable, Pedersen found explained in phonotactic terms, sentence sandhi.

And it seems to me that, however theoretically unsatisfactory and disquieting their conclusion may be, Wackernagel and Pedersen are correct in deriving all forms showing final -/a/ in European languages from IE-*/a/, regardless of whether Sanskrit has -/a/ or -/i/. Pedersen's conditioning factor, however, is not sufficient, being only a guess, for one wonders why -/a/ should remain -/a/ before a pause but pass to -/i/ in sentence sandhi. It is impossible for us at this distance in time to determine which was the prepausal form, and even whether final position in the sentence had any affect on vowel color. Since we cannot know about these things, we must discard Pedersen's attempt at providing phonological conditioning, or at least hold it in abeyance because itself requiring explanation and justification. It is best simply to admit (with Wackernagel) that no phonological conditioning is discernible. But we can at least state one thing about the distribution of unaccented -/a/ and -/i/ which is not subject to dispute: -/a/ occurs in the singular of the perfect active, and only in the singular of the perfect active, while -/i/ occurs everywhere else. Since we can specify the morphological environment, we are free to suppose that the morphological, not the phonological, environment is relevant in stating the distribution of word-final -/a/. And we can then state in rule form: unaccented -/a/ passes to -/i/ except in the singular perfect active.

Those who feel that morphological considerations can affect phonological developments will have no difficulty in accepting this type of explanation, while those who allow only phonological conditioning for sound change will of course be unable to accept it.[19] To answer objections from this quarter, I will state first that the rule given above seems almost inevitably demanded by the data, for setting up a new phonological entity solely to account for two morphological elements is most uneconomical. And though I shall not in fact provide a truly satisfactory explanation, I would suggest that certain factors were at work other than simply that **woida* and **woitstha* are perfect forms.

There is the fairly strong possibility that the second singular ending of the perfect is the same originally as the ending of the first person plural middle, that is to say, in both cases */dha/. But in the one case the */dha/ passed to /dhi/ in Sanskrit, in the other it did not. The reason, or a reason, for this divergence may well be the fact that -/dha/ of */medha/ was not opposed to any other ending *-medh-*, while *-dha* of the second singular perfect active was opposed to the *-dhi* of the imperative. To be sure the vocalism of the root differed, *οἶσθα* beside *ἴσθι*, but there was nonetheless an opposition in the ending lacking in the first plural middle. And this fact leads us to consider the morphological role of the -/a/ in the other sure case in which it occurs, in the neuter plural. We have already seen that the -/a/ here is secondary, not originally part of the ending, and that it was added in Sanskrit to counteract the tendency toward loss of final nasals and stops. And in Greek the regular phonological development of **bherōnt* would have been *φέρον*, the same form as the neuter singular. Hence the -/a/ in Greek (originally) served only to protect the -/t/ and was not itself the mark of the plural: the long vowel marked plurality. Nor was *-/a/ the mark of the first person plural middle: it served only to prevent Gk. **φέρομε*<**bheromedh* and Skt. **bharāmat*<**bheromedh*. And the -/a/ of **ita* also lacked morphological significance. We can thus state that morphologically insignificant -/a/ passes to /i/.[20]

The -/a/ of **woid(h)a* was grammatically relevant, and was the only phonological device which served to distinguish **woid(h)a* from **woide*, but also from possible confusion with other middle forms in *-i*. We may thus rephrase our rule by extending it to cover all grammatically relevant forms rather than specifically forms of the perfective aspect, though it is only here that the rule has an opportunity to be applied. And perhaps, in order to make the rule slightly more palatable to those who require phonological conditioning, we may suppose that grammatically relevant forms, if not exactly stressed, were at least not unstressed either, and held a somewhat middle position between stressed and unstressed. They were not stressed to be sure, but were not unstressed. Hence on this interpretation the rule for Indo-Iranian is: -/a/ passes (to [ə]) to /i/ in unstressed open syllables, but remains elsewhere. But I prefer to avoid such questionable phonology and to assume that: */a/ in unstressed open syllables passes to I-I /i/ save when grammatically relevant.[21]

This part of the argument, then, is over: */a/ between consonants or between consonant and pause remains when accented or when in a closed syllable, otherwise it passes to I-I Ø initially, /i/ elsewhere. Perhaps, though, it would be well at this point to provide gross total figures for the different developments of */a/ in various positions. These figures will show that there is, if not an absolute unanimity in forms conforming to my rules, there is at least a statistical bias in favor of assuming only */a/ and not both */a/ and */ə/. In the table I give maximum figures for each situation, and do not take into account the refinements made above which involved dismissing a number of apparent exceptions. In other words the totals include every instance numbered or counted in the body of the text. Only those forms relegated to the Appendix are not counted. From the table it will be clear that there are 91 positive instances and only 14 negative, a ratio of about 6:1.

	Positive			*Negative*	
	á	ə̆	Ø	ă	ə́
#_C—	21	—	12	7	0
—C_C—	34	16	—	3	2
—C_C#	2	1	—	0	0
—C_#	1	4	—	2	0
Total	58	21	12	12	2
	91			14	

The rules formulated thus far handle cases of */a/ after a consonant, but make no provision for */a/ after a vowel. We have seen above that in nonfinal syllables unaccented */a/ appears as length after /i/ or */u/ as in the cases mentioned there (above p. 24), and in:[22]

īnkhati 'moves up and down' <**i-ankh-* 'mixes, stirs up' (with I-I root *ankh-;* M. I.20, 95).

ī́jati 'sets in motion' <**i-ag-* (M. I.95).

īrtsati 'wishes to increase', reduplicated desiderative to *ṛdhati* <**i-aldh-* (M. I.124).

pratīpaḥ 'adverse opposite' <**proti* + *ap-* 'water' (M. II.361).

And it is quite clear that it appears as length also in final position, as in the cases mentioned on page 16, and also in:

Skt. *patnī* 'mistress, wife', Gk. πότνια 'mistress' <**potnia* (M. II.202–03, F. II.586–587, Szemerényi 1964a:391–395).

Skt. *áśrū(ni)* 'tears', Gk. δάκρυα 'id.' <*(*d*)*akrua.*

The rule can thus be stated very simply and very generally for the development of IE */a/. It remains /a/ in the European languages, but develops in Indo-Iranian as follows:

$$/a/ > /i/ \quad /C\,\_\_\_ \begin{bmatrix} \# \\ C \end{bmatrix}$$

$$> /{:}/ \quad /V\,\_\_\_ \begin{bmatrix} \# \\ C \end{bmatrix}$$

$$> /a/ \text{ elsewhere, i.e. } \begin{bmatrix} RC \\ \acute{\_\_} \end{bmatrix}$$

There is thus no need or call to contrast [a] and [ə] in Indo-European: they are allophones of the same phoneme /a/.

And if [a] and [ə] are allophones of /a/, then clearly there is no reason to suppose that [ə] became an allophone of /a/ only after having developed from an earlier laryngeal /H/. That conclusion rested on distributional statements regarding /H/, namely that it appeared as [h] initially, [:] after vowels (save sometimes in Hittite), and as [ə] between consonants. If we want (for reasons which will have to remain obscure to me) to retain this analysis, we shall now have to assume a rule:

/H/ > [ə]/C ˘ C
[:]/V ___
[h]/___ V
[a]/ [´ C
___ RC]

a rule that will encounter difficulties before a vowel, and which is unmotivated by the comparative evidence. Hence, though /h/ may well have been part of the IE phonemic inventory (Wyatt 1964: 149, Szemerényi 1967: 89–90), it did not appear between consonants as [ə], and our guesses as to the nature of prior stages of Indo-European should henceforth feature fewer *h*'s. But there should be more */a/.

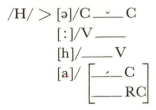

Appendix I

Since it is customary in discussions of IE phonology to make a guess as to the nature of earlier stages of Indo-European, I shall make one here, obviously not in the hope of settling the question, but rather as a pledge to the sincerity of my proposals and to forestall possible objections leveled at my proposals based on presumed earlier stages of Indo-European. And I shall be able to account further for the comparative rarity of */a/ in our PIE reconstructions. In what follows I restrict myself to the short vowel system, though long vowels and diphthongs could easily be accommodated, and in fact per force enter in later on. In my discussion I shall employ the symbols PIE, PPIE, PPPIE: PIE will stand for the language reconstructed on the basis of cognate sets in the various IE languages; PPIE will stand for the language (or de rigueur, the vocalic system) which lies immediately behind PIE; and PPPIE is the stage anterior to PPIE, the earliest system of IE vowels for which we have any evidence at all. The number of P's will be matched by the number of asterisks when hypothetical forms are cited: e.g. ***ág- > **ág- > *ág-.

It seems that Indo-European always had the five short vowels /i e a o u/, whatever else it may have had, and that these vowels could appear both accented and unaccented; the accent seems to have had a strong stress component. The PPPIE system contained.

	accented					*unaccented*				
	i				u	i				u
PPPIE		e		o			e		o	
			a					a		

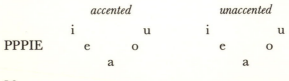

Later the unaccented mid-vowels disappeared through vowel syncope, at least in open syllables and in words of more than two syllables, and there resulted (in PPIE) a tripartite opposition in unaccented syllables: the five-vowel system remained in accented syllables.[23]

	accented					*unaccented*		
	i				u	i		u
PPIE		e		o				
			a				a	

At this point, the immediately preablaut, and hence immediately pre-IE period, /a i u/ could appear both accented and unaccented, /e o/ could appear only accented. As a result of a grammaticalization of this accentual relation, accent came to imply /e/ or /o/, /a i u/ implied unaccented position, and /e/ and /o/ were introduced into accented positions where they previously had not been, notably in the present tense (imperfective aspect) of verbs and other categories later characterized by the /e/-grade. Only well-established words, words of high frequency such as ***ág-* 'set in motion' were able to resist this tendency. The reason that /e/ was felt to characterize the present (imperfective) seems to be that there were in Indo-European several words of imperfective meaning which contained the vowel /e/ in their root, verbs like ***bhero-* ***bhers* ***bhert* ***bherm(e)* ***bhert(e)* ***bhernt* (cf. Lat. *fero fers fert ferimus ferte ferunt*), a verb which may have had an earlier paradigm ****bhero-* ****bheres* ****bheret* etc.

When society became sufficiently complex that it was no longer possible to utilize separate words (suppletive paradigms) for semantically related but aspectually different concepts, the vowel /e/ was inserted between the first two consonants of the root (if there were two initial consonants). That is to say, old "paradigms" such as 'say' *φημί ἐρῶ εἶπον* in Greek became inefficient and cumbersome and tended to be replaced by more regular paradigms like λέγω λέξω ἔλεξα. There were other such devices, but the insertion of /e/ was at this stage the most productive one. Hence to a root ***sghó-* 'have, take' (which may or may not have come from ****seghó-*) with the paradigm **sghóm **sghés **sghé(t) **sghóm(e) **sghét(e) *sghón(t)* there was formed a new paradigm *séghoa (with -/a/ from the perfect ??) > *segho:, *séghes(i) *séghet(i) *séghom(e) *séghet(e) séghont(i)* after verbs like *bhéro:. Because this new imperfective paradigm had a vowel before the final consonant, a vowel was introduced in the ending of most original imperfectives so that **bhéro: **bhérs **bhért became *bhéro: *bhéres(i) *bhéret(i). Only relics like Lat. *fero fers fert* as opposed to Skt. *bhárāmi bhárasi bhárati* and verbs of frequent occurrence like 'to be' held out against this trend.

If imperfective (etc.) forms were created to unaccented roots containing /i/ or /u/ such as **lik^{w}- in **lik^{w}ó- 'I leave', they took the shape *léik^{w}o-, *lelóik^{w}a rather than *líík^{w}o-, *lelíík^{w}a.[24] Presumably it was this insertion of an accented vowel before another vowel (or semivowel) which converted the old stress system of accentuation into the late IE pitch-accent system, the system continued in Vedic Sanskrit and Greek. And this new system of accentuation which opposed unaccented to rising and rising to falling (e.g. in *léik^{w}-) tended to preserve unaccented vowels and did not allow them to be lost through syncope.[25]

But if the verb contained a vowel other than /i/ or /u/ in what subsequently became (or remained) the imperfective aspect, the insertion of the vowel /e/ resulted in a long vowel, if the root began with a single consonant or a stop consonant preceded by /s/, as in *dhe:- 'place', the original root of which must have been **dhe- with the imperfective paradigm:

PPPIE	>	PPIE	>	PIE
(CV)dhém(i)		(CV)dhémi		(CV)dhéemi = dhe:mi
(CV)dhés(i)		(CV)dhési		(CV)dhéesi = dhe:si
(CV)dhét(i)		(CV)dhéti		(CV)dhéeti = dhe:ti
(CV)dhemé		(CV)dhmé		(CV)dhmé
(CV)dheté		(CV)dhté		(CV)dhté
(CV)dhént(i)		(CV)dhénti		(CV)dhénti

The PIE situation is exactly mirrored in the Skt. paradigm which shows 1st sg. *dádhāmi,* 1st plur. *dadhmáḥ* beside the remodeled *dádhāmaḥ*. Gk. had remodeled the 1st and 2d plural forms after the 3d plural already before our earliest records. **sista:mi* derives from **sísteami*, 1st plur. *sistamé* (to a root **sta-*), and this verb together with **dídhe:mi* set up the IE pattern: long vowel in singular, no vowel (or /a/) in plural which changed **dídeumi* (<**dídeomi*): *didmé* 'give' to **dídoomi* (=**dído:mi*): **didmé* (seen in Skt. *dádāmi, dadmáḥ*). This same relation ultimately accounted for the change of Gk. **deikneumi* : *deiknumen* to δείκνῡμι : δείκνυμεν.

In other cases /é/ may have replaced /á/, as in the examples mentioned above (p. 41). But when the root consisted of a consonant cluster plus vowel rather than of single consonant (symbol TRV), the /é/ or /ó/ was frequently inserted between the consonants, thus giving rise to disyllabic roots. Such roots were then of the shape *Te/oRV-* beside *TRe/oV-*. Thus from ***tla-* 'lift, bear' there was formed an allomorph **téla-* (seen in τελαμών 'carrying-strap') beside the other allomorph **tlea-* > **tla:-* (in τέτλᾱκα 'I have endured', Lat. *lātus* 'carried'). The later disyllabic roots, then, were simply adaptations to the new scheme of things of old roots ending in -/a/.[26]

The preceding sketch is obviously just that, a sketch, and is far from being a complete account of the origins of IE verbal root structure: it is intended merely to point the way and to suggest possibilities for reconstruction opened up by the identification of /a/ and schwa. I do not pretend to have faced, let alone answered, all the myriad problems my position entails. What is more, my remarks are by the very nature of the case somewhat fanciful, and are at least in part intended also to forestall some criticisms which might be leveled by those who feel that /ə/ (or /H/) is demanded by the requirements, if not of comparative reconstruction, at least of IE root structure. Neither /ə/ nor /H/ is required by theoretical considerations, and I hope to have shown that /a/ is.

Appendix II

In this appendix I gather together all those cases which I have found for which IE */a/ in positions other than initial has been proposed by various scholars in the past. There are several categories into which these words can be fit: 1) words which may in fact show IE */a/ but which cannot be used to establish */a/ because they are either a) nursery words or b) onomatopoeic; 2) words which might be related and which have been proposed as examples of */a/, but which are unlikely because of some phonological difficulty or on semantic grounds; 3) words which, though proposed at some time in the past, cannot be related, or at least are most unlikely to be related. Clearly there will be some overlap between 2) and 3), and in general I include in 2) only those instances for which a protoform can be reconstructed. I number cases in 1) and 2) *1ff. to show that they might be added to the instances of */a/ given in the body of the text. Words listed in 3) will be numbered †1ff.: they cannot be added to the list of more or less well-established cases of */a/.

1a) Nursery words (Pedersen 1900:83)

*1. Skt. *tatáḥ* 'father', Gk. *τάτα*, Lat. *tata,* Russ. *táta* (M. II.471, W-H II.650). Turkish has *ata.*

*2. Skt. *nanā́* 'mother', Gk. *νάννα* 'aunt' (M. II.304 "reduplizierte Lallwort", F. II.131 "Lallwort")

1b) Onomatopoeic formations

*3. Skt. *balbalākaroti* 'bégayer', Lat. *balbus* 'bégue'; Skt. *barbaraḥ* 'stammering', Gk. *βάρβαρος* 'foreign'

(M. II.411–412, 420, F. I.219–220, W-H I.94, Kuryłowicz 1956:190)

*4. Skt. *gañjanaḥ* 'despising, contemning', Gk. *γαγγαίνειν· τὸ μετὰ γέλωτος προσπαίζειν* (Hes.), OE *cancettan* 'railer', OCS *gǫgnǫti* 'murmurer' (M. I.315, F. I.281, Kuryłowicz 1956:190). Frisk seems to accept connection of the Gk. and Skt. forms, but Mayrhofer feels that, since the Skt. word appears for the first time in the Middle Ages, it is not to be compared with the Gk. and OE forms. Kuryłowicz feels that the words are onomatopoeic in origin.

*5. Skt. *carkarti* 'makes mention of, praises', Gk. *καρκαίρω* 'quake' (LSJ), *ἐκάρκαιρον·ψόφον τινὰ ἀπετέλουν* (Hes.), Lat. *carmen* 'song', ON *hrōđr* 'Ruhm, Lob' (M. I.377, F. I.789, W-H I.169–170). The Lat. form at least is not to be compared here, for it derives from **can-men* to *canere* 'sing'. Frisk, in comparing the Skt. form, treats the word as originally onomatopeoic.

*6. Skt. *kokiláḥ* 'the Indian cuckoo', Gk. *καυκαλίας*, a kind of bird, *καύαξ*, a seabird (M. I.268–269, F. I.801–802, Kuryłowicz 1956:189). Both Mayrhofer and Frisk take these words as onomatopoeic, but Kuryłowicz, comparing Lith. *kaũkti* 'heurler' and Skt. *káuti* 'cries', feels that all these words may derive from a long-diphthongal form.

*7. Skt. *króśati* 'shrieks', Gk. *κραυγή* 'crying, screaming', Goth. *hrukjan* 'chanter (coq)' (M. I.281, F. II.10–11, Kuryłowicz 1956:189). Both Frisk and Mayrhofer stress the onomatopoeic nature of these words, a fact mentioned also by Kuryłowicz, but he favors derivation from a long-diphthongal root because of Lith. *krokiù, krõkti* 'râler' and other forms which point to **krā-*.

*8. Skt. *kákhati* 'laughs', Gk. *καχάζω* 'laugh aloud', Lat. *cachinno* 'laugh aloud' (M. I.136, F. I.804, W-H I.126, E-M 80, Kuryłowicz 1956:190). All authorities recognize that these words are sound-imitative, and only Ernout-Meillet consider them derived from an IE word. Kuryłowicz, however, objects that they cannot be, since Gk. χ cannot correspond to Skt. /kh/ save after /s/.

*9. Skt. *lalallā* "onomatopoetisch vom Laut eines Lallers" (M.), Gk. λαλέω 'talk, prattle', λάλος 'talkative', Lat. *lallo* 'sing lalla' (M. III.92, F. II.77, W-H I.752–753, Kuryłowicz 1956:190).

*10. Interjections such as those mentioned by Kuryłowicz (1956:190): Skt. *uvé,* Ave. *vayōi, avōi,* Lat. *vae,* Gaul. *gwae,* Goth. *wai,* Lett. *vai.*

2) The second category consists of correspondences which, though not excluded theoretically as was the case with 1), are not acceptable as certain instances of /a/ because of some phonological or semantic weakness in the equation.

*11. Skt. *bálam* 'power, strength, might', comparative and superlative *bálīyān, báliṣṭhaḥ,* Lat. *dēbilis* 'weak', OCS *bolijь* 'grösser, besser', Gk. *βέλτερος, βέλτιστος* 'better, best' (Pedersen 1900:82, M. II.416–418, F. I.232, W-H I.326–327). This word can be considered to contain IE /a/ only if Phryg. *βαλήν* 'king', OIr. *balc* 'strong', Welsh *balch* are related; and if Gk. *βέλτερος* is a replacement for an earlier **βάλτερος*; and if the Skt. word is not a Dravidian loan, as has been held by some (Burrow 1946:19, denied by Thieme 1955:447). The Lat. word is not related, since it derives from *dēbeo.*

*12. Skt. *dhánvan-* 'bow', Ger. *Tanne* 'fir-tree' (M. II.90–91, Pedersen 1900:82, Thieme 1953:550–551). Pedersen is reluctant to adopt this comparison because the relationship of the meanings is very distant. Thieme makes the strongest case for the connection.

*13. Skt. *bhanákti* 'breaks', Lat. *frango* 'break' (M. II.469, W-H I.541, E-M 251–252, Pedersen 1900:78). This comparison is valid only if Skt. *giri-bhráj-*, of uncertain meaning (M. II.527), is related. But even at that all other evidence points to a root **bheg-/*bheng-* (Mayrhofer).

*14. Skt. *bráhman-* 'Formung, Gestaltung', Lat. *flāmen* 'priest' (M. II.452–456, W-H I.512–513, E-M 239, Pedersen 1900:82, Puhvel 1964:1–7). The Latin form is more likely to be related to various Germanic words such as Goth. *blōtan* 'verehren'.

*15. Skt. *davaḥ* 'Brand', *doman-* 'Brand, Qual' to *dunóti* 'burns', Gk. *δαίω*, *δεδαυμένος* 'kindle' (M. II.49, F. I.342–343, P. 179–181).

*16. Skt. *gábhastiḥ* 'arm, hand; beam of light', Lat. *habeo* 'have, hold' (Güntert 1916:8). There is nothing to recommend this equation.

*17. Skt. *kalikā* 'bud', Gk. *κάλυξ* 'cup of a flower' (M. I.181, F. I.768, Pedersen 1900:77).

*18. Skt. *śarkaraḥ* 'Kiesel, Stein', Lat. *calx* 'small stone used in gaming' (U. 305, F. I.22, W-H I.145, E-M 89, Pedersen, 1900:78). The Lat. word is probably a borrowing of Gk. *χάλιξ* 'small stone', and the Skt. word may well be related to Gk. *κροκάλη* 'seashore'.

*19. Skt. *karparaḥ* 'cup, pot', Gk. *κάλπη* 'pitcher' (M. I.174, F. I.767–768, Pedersen 1900:77). Frisk is probably right in holding that the Gk. word is 'wie so viele Gefässnamen ohne sichere Erklärung': he does not mention the Skt. form.

*20. Skt. *kámpate* 'trembles', Gk. *κάμπτω* 'bend', Lat. *campus* 'plain, field', Lith. *kam̃pas* 'Winkel' (M. I.160, F. I.775,

W-H I.148–149). All these forms can easily derive from a **kamp-*, but the semantic connection is weak.

*21. Skt. *candráḥ* 'shining, Moon', *cándati* 'shines', Gk. *κάνδαρος·ἄνθραξ*, Lat. *candidus* 'white', Gaul. *cann* 'brilliant' (M. I.373, F. I.776, W-H I.151–152, E-M 92). The Skt. form points to an original **kend-* because of its palatalization, but this may be an innovation. All other forms point to **kand-*.

*22. Skt. *kandaraḥ* 'cave, glen', Gk. *κάνδαλοι·κοιλώματα, βάθρα* (Hes.). Mayrhofer (I.152) hesitates between this connection and connection with *kakundaram* of Asiatic origin. Frisk does not discuss the Gk. word.

*23. Skt. *kapā́lam* 'cup, skull', Lat. *caput,* 'head', OE *hafola* 'Head' (M. I.155, W-H I.163–164, E-M 99, Pedersen 1900:77). There does seem to have been an IE root **kap-* 'head', variously extended in the various languages. But it must have been accented, and the OE form proves the Skt. accent secondary.

*24. Skt. *káp̣ṛt(h)* 'penis', Gk. *κάπρος* 'boar', Lat. *caper* 'he-goat' (M. I.157, F. I.783, W-H I.157).

*25. Skt. *kapaṭī* 'zwei handvoll', Lat. *capio* 'take' (M. I.154, W-H I.159–160, E-M 97, Pedersen 1900:77). There seems no reason to connect these words, and Mayrhofer suspects the Skt. form to be connected with *kavalaḥ* 'a mouthful, morsel', and of non-Aryan origin.

*26. Skt. *śaphá* 'hoof', OHG *huof* 'hoof' (P. 530, U. 303, Pedersen 1900:82, Mayrhofer 1952:27). Mayrhofer accepts the equation, but it is most unlikely because the words point to different vocalic lengths in Indo-European. Furthermore one must not ignore OCS *kopyto* 'hoof' which must also be related, though pointing to a different type of IE *k*. Rather all these words must be of onomatopoeic origin.

*27. Skt. *śásti, śásati* 'cuts', Gk. *κεάζω* 'split', Lat. *castro* 'castrate' (P. 586, U. 306–307, F. I.806, W-H I.179–180, E-M 104, Pedersen 1900:82). The Lat. form is the only one pointing to an original /a/.

*28. Skt. *śátruḥ* 'enemy', OIr. *cath* 'lutte', PGmc. **haþu* (P. 534, F. I.931, Mayrhofer 1952:27, Kuryłowicz 1956:191). IE **ḱat-* is rendered unlikely on the one hand by Gk. *κότος* 'resentment' and OCS *kotora* 'Kampf'.

*29. Skt. *śávīraḥ* 'puissant', OIr. *caur* 'héros', Welsh *cawr* 'géant' (P. 592–594, U. 306, F. II.54, Kuryłowicz 1956:191). Skt. *śū́raḥ* 'fort, vaillant, héros' and Gk. *κύριος* 'having power or authority' combine to make it seem likely that the Skt. form is secondary, formed on the analogy of *bhū-*:*bhávitum,* and thus not directly comparable with the Celtic forms.

*30. Skt. *krátuḥ* 'power, understanding', Gk. *κράτος* 'strength', *κρατύς* 'strong' (P. 531, M. I.276, F. II.9–10). All other Gk. forms point to */e/.

*31. Skt. *lavíḥ, lavítra-* 'sickle' to *lunā́ti* 'cuts', Gk. *λαῖον* 'ploughshare' (M. III.93, F. II.73, Kuryłowicz 1956:191). The Skt. forms are attested late only, and are almost certainly late derivatives of *lunā́ti,* and hence not comparable with Gk. *λαῖον*.

*32. Skt. *kṣatrám* 'might, power', Lat. *satelles* 'attendant' (M. I.285, W-H II.481, E-M 595, Pedersen 1900:82). This comparison was discarded by Pedersen because the semantic difficulties were too great. *Satelles* is in fact most likely an Etruscan loan-word.

*33. Skt. *kṣáyati* 'rules, possesses', Gk. *κτάομαι* 'get' (M. I.287, F. II.30–33). Mayrhofer favors connection, Frisk is opposed.

*34. Skt. *lambate* 'sinkt', Lat. *lābor* 'slide', *labo* 'begin to sink' (M. III.44, W-H II.739, E-M 333–334, Pedersen 1900:78).

*35. Ave. *masyå* 'grösser', *masō* 'Grösse', Gk. *μακρός* 'long' (F. II.164–165, 224–225, Pedersen 1900:82–83).

*36. Skt. *mandiram* 'dwelling, house', *mandurā́* 'Pferdestall', Gk. *μάνδρα* 'enclosed space' (M. II.582, F. II.169, Kuryłowicz 1956:192). All these scholars connect these words, but all also assume borrowing and that the word is not of IE origin.

*37. Skt. *mañjúḥ* 'beautiful', *mañjuláḥ* 'id.', Gk. *μάγγανον* 'philtre', OPruss. *manga* 'courtisane' (M. II.553, F. II.155, W-H II.28–29, Kuryłowicz 1956:191). Mayrhofer feels that the Skt. form is not likely to be related to European forms, and suggests Dravidian connections.

*38. Skt. *médaḥ* 'fat, marrow', Gk. *μαζός* 'breast', OHG *mast* 'Futter, Mästung' (P. 694–695, M. II.683–684, F. II.183).

*39. Skt. *salilám* 'Meer, Meerflut', Gk. *ἅλς* 'salt', Lat. *sāl* 'id.' (F. I.78–79, W-H II.465–466, Thieme 1953:561–562). That there was a European word **sal-* 'salt' there can be no doubt. That **sal-* was Indo-European also depends on whether one accepts Thieme's identification with this root of Skt. *salilám*.

*40. Skt. *uccalati* 'springs upward', Gk. *ἅλλομαι* 'spring', Lat. *salio* 'leap' (M. I.99, F. I.76, W-H II.468, Pedersen 1900:83). Mayrhofer favors connection with a root **ḱel-* seen in Germ. *beschälen* 'cover, horse (a mare)'.

*41. Skt. *sasyám* 'blés, grains', Gaul. *sasiam* (transmitted as *asiam*) 'seigle', Welsh *haidd* 'hordeum' (P. 880, U. 332, W-H I.72, Kuryłowicz 1956:191). Agricultural terms of this sort, especially if restricted to geographically distant areas of the IE domain, are far from secure.

*42. Skt. *śoṣaḥ* 'qui dessèche; sécheresse', Gk. *αὖος* 'dry' (U. 317, F. I.189, Kuryłowicz 1956:191). These words are clearly related, but cannot be used as evidence for /a/ because as Frisk says the Skt. form, though formally identical, is to be considered a late verbal noun to *śúṣyati:* it appears late, and differs from the Gk. form in meaning.

3) The third category consists of words which, with a few possible exceptions, cannot be used as evidence of IE /a/, though they have been in the past.

†1. Skt. *bhadráḥ* 'fortunate, blessed', Goth. *batiza* 'better' (P. 106, M. II.467, Pedersen 1900:82). Though the etymology of the Skt. word is not certain, it does seem (with Mayrhofer) to be connected with *bhándate* 'is praised', and hence stems from an earlier **bhn̥dró-*.

†2. Skt. *gádhyaḥ* 'was man gerne festhält' to a root *gadh-*, OFris. *gadia* 'vereinigen', Germ. *Gatte* 'husband', OCS *godъ* 'Zeit', Toch. *kātk-* 'sich erfreuen' (P. 423–424, M. I.320–321, Güntert 1916:8). These words are so remote semantically and formally that they are not likely even to be related. But if they are, a root **ghedh-*/ **ghodh-* will account for them.

†3. Skt. *gáhvaraḥ* 'deep', Gk. *βῆσσα* 'wooded glen' (P. 465, M. I.332, F. I.234, Pedersen 1900:77, Schwyzer 1932: 193–203, Szemerényi 1960:211–216). The vowels do not agree, and if the equation is to be kept, then Gk. *βαθύς* 'deep' must be brought in. But it, because of *βάθος* 'depth' and *βένθος* 'depth', points unequivocally to an earlier **bendh-*/**bn̥dh-*.

†4. Skt. *śaknóti* 'be able', Germ. *behagen* 'suit, please' (P. 522, U. 301, Pedersen 1900:82). Again the semantic link is weak, and if made, does not exclude a root **ḱek-*/**ḱok-*.

†5. Skt. *kakúbh-, kakúd-* 'peak, summit', Lat. *cacūmen* 'summit' (M. I.135, W-H I.127, E-M 81, Pedersen 1900: 77, Kuryłowicz 1956:190). Though this equation is quite frequently made, it is impossible. As Kuryłowicz (1956:192) points out, the words are quite differently formed : the Indic suffix is secondary, the Lat. primary. And within Indic it is difficult to ignore the words *kākút* 'palate' and *kākuḥ* 'cry of lamentation', both of which may be related, if we can assume *kakúdmant* to have passed through a semantic development: 'having voice' > 'head' > 'summit'.

†6. Skt. *khálaḥ* 'threshing-floor', Arm. *kal* 'id.' (Pedersen 1900:82). But Mayrhofer (I.305) finds the Skt. form 'nicht sicher erklärt', and Thieme (1955:439) feels that it is the 'vernacular counterfeit of the educated form *khara*'.

†7. Skt. *khalīnam* 'bit of a bridle', Gk. *χαλινός* 'bridle' (Güntert 1916:8). But the Skt. word is clearly a loan from Gk. (M. I.306).

†8. Skt. *kapúcchalam* 'tuft of hair on the hind part of the head', Lat. *caput* 'head' (M. I.156, W-H I.163–164, Kuryłowicz 1956:190). But the Skt. form is not to be analyzed *kaput-śala,* but as *ka-puccha-la* with the pejorative prefix *ka-* (Mayrhofer, Kuryłowicz).

†9. Skt. *kapíḥ* 'monkey', cf. Gk. *κῆπος* 'monkey' (Pedersen 1900:77). Though it is likely enough that the words are related, it is further likely that Gk. *κῆβος* and Hebrew *qōph* are also related (M. I.156, F. I.836), and that therefore the word is borrowed into both Greek and Sanskrit and is not of IE date, a supposition rendered the more likely by the nature of the animal designated.

†10. Skt. *kapíḥ* 'olibanum', Gk. *καπνός* 'smoke' (P. 596–597, Pedersen 1900:77). Mayrhofer (I.156) feels that the numerous by-forms in Sanskrit plus the fact that the

word is not attested in literature is sufficient almost to exclude the possibility of IE origin. Frisk (I.781–782) does not mention the Skt. word.

†11. Skt. *kapanā* 'caterpillar', Gk. *κάμπη* 'id.' (Pedersen 1900:77, M. I.154, F. I.774). The equation is possible, but only on the assumption of an earlier **kemp* ∼ **kmp*, with the Gk. form remodeled after *κάμπτω*.

†12. Skt. *śásman* 'invocation', Lat. *carmen* 'song' (W-H I.169–170, Pedersen 1900:82). Pedersen discarded this equation, proposed by others, because Lat. *-sm-* does not pass to *-rm-*. See above *5.

†13. Skt. *kvathati* 'boils', Lat. *cāseus* 'cheese' (P. 627, M. I.283, W-H I.176–177). The forms are too unlike phonologically to be compared and to provide evidence for an IE original.

†14. Skt. *kharaḥ* 'hard, rough', Gk. *κάρχαρος*, *καρχάλεος* 'sawlike', 'rough' (M. I.302, F. I.796, Kuryłowicz 1956:189). Kuryłowicz holds that this equation is to be discarded because Skt. *kh-* cannot correspond to Gk. *χ*.

†15. NPers. *lab* 'lip', Lat. *labrum* 'id.' (Pedersen 1900:83). Pedersen also points out that /e/-forms of this word occur, as in Germ. *Lippe*.

†16. Skt. *marúḥ* 'wilderness', Lat. *mare* 'sea' (M. II.591–592, W-H II.38–39, E-M 387, Pedersen 1900:82). Pedersen feels that a closer agreement in stem-form is demanded for words so semantically distant. E-M deny that there is a Skt. cognate to Lat. *mare*.

†17. Skt. *pajráḥ* 'solid', Gk. *πήγνυμι* 'stick in, fix in' (M. II.186, F. II.525–526, Pedersen 1900:82). Frisk does not even mention the Skt. form, and Mayrhofer indicates that the meaning of the Skt. word is not certain.

†18. Skt. *pastíyam* 'dwelling', Arm. *hast* 'fixed', ON *fastr*, OE *fæst* (M. II.242, Kuryłowicz 1956:191). Again the

meaning of the Skt. form is not completely certain, and if assured, then, as Kuryłowicz says, the semantic link between the Skt. and the European forms is weak.

†19. Skt. *rádati* 'bites', Lat. *rādo* 'scrape' (M. III.39–40, W-H II.415, E-M 563, Pedersen 1900:83). Though it is likely that the words are related, they cannot be directly equated phonologically.

†20. Skt. *ríṣyati, réṣati* 'be hurt, injured', Gk. *ῥαίω* 'break, smash' (M. III.62, B. 833, Kuryłowicz 1956:191, 192). Mayrhofer does not even mention this equation, and Kuryłowicz says it is suspect because of the lack of prothesis in Greek.

†21. Skt. *sabardhúk* 'Neumelk', OHG *saf* 'sap', or Gk. *ἄφαρ* 'straightway, forthwith' (U. 328, F. I.194, Pedersen 1900:83). There is no reason to consider this equation.

†22. Skt. *sraj-* 'chain, wreath', Lat. *frāgum* 'strawberry'. This comparison was discarded by Pedersen (1900:82).

†23. Skt. *vagnúḥ* 'call, cry', Lat. *vāgīre* 'cry, squall' (M. III.123, F. II.513, I.646–647, W-H II.725–726, E-M 711). The discrepancy in quantity excludes this comparison, a comparison which would, if correct, be a case of onomatopoeia anyway.

†24. Skt. *vañjulaḥ* 'calamus rotang', Lat. *vagāri* 'stroll about' (M. III.128, W-H II.726–727, E-M 711, Kuryłowicz 1956:189).

†25. Skt. *api-vátati* 'understand', Lat. *vātēs* 'seer' (M. III.132, W-H II.737–738, E-M 715, Pedersen 1900:77). The Lat. word is almost certainly related to Western European words like OIr. *fáith* 'poet', and not to *apivátati.*

†26. Skt. *yátati* 'attach', Gk. *ζητέω* 'seek' (M. III.5, F. I.613, Pedersen 1900:77). But *ζητέω* derives from a root **diā-* seen in the reduplicated *δίζημι* 'seek out'.

Inevitably there will be dispute about my classification, and indeed about a number of cases included in the text. Some will feel that I have been too generous in admitting cognates, others that I have been too ready to exclude possible instances. I myself feel that of the cognate pairs included in 2) the following have a fair chance of actually being related: *15 *daw-* 'burn', *20 *kamp-* 'bend', *21 *kand-* 'shine', *24 *kapr-* 'penis', *30 *kratus,* 'power', *42 *sausos* 'dry', though here the forms may not be equatable directly on the phonological level. The following seem most unlikely: *12 *dhanw-* 'fir', *16 *ghabh-* 'hold', *25 **kap-* 'take', *32 *ksat-* '?', these for primarily semantic reasons; *13 *bh(r)an-* 'break', *26 *kap-* 'hoof', these for phonological reasons. It does not seem possible that any of the cases in 3) can be seriously considered.

Whether or not one is inclined to accept any of the cases in 2) as reliable cognates, it is interesting that almost all conform to my rules, so that they at least cannot invalidate my hypothesis. Only *23 *kap-,* *26 *kap-,* *32 *ksat-,* *41 *sasi-* 'grain' fail to conform, and we have seen that *26 and *32 are not seriously to be considered. Only *23 *kap-* 'head' and *41 *sasi-* 'grain' remain. I think it would not be unfair to conclude that no cases in 2) or 3) are of sufficient weight or importance to invalidate my assumption that unaccented */a/ > [ə].

Notes

[1] For the history of the IE vocalic system, cf. Pedersen (1931:240–310), Szemerényi (1964:2–6, 1967:67–69), Wyatt (1964:141–144); and for the history of laryngeal analyses of that system, Polomé (1965:9–78).

[2] I here follow de Saussure (1922:168–169) and Kuryłowicz (1956:201–208) in regarding only Gk. /a/ as the regular reflex of IE *[ə]. For a fuller (but still inadequate) discussion of the problem see below fn. 15.

[3] The table does not include all the possible sources of /e/ and /o/ in the daughter languages, but is sufficient for the argument here presented. For the record, though, laryngealists hold that /e/ can derive from both */e/ and */H_1e/, while /o/ can come from */o/, */H_3e/, */H_1o/, and */H_3o/.

[4] Burrow objected to [ə] on other grounds as well (1949:28–29). He found it difficult to imagine that European [a] and I-I [i], phonetically distant sounds, should both have derived from [ə]; and that [ə] > [a] independently in all European languages. But if, as I shall propose, [ə] develops from IE */a/, both these objections are answered, and we have only to explain (as we shall below) how I-I /i/ < /a/. His objections do have force, though, when applied to laryngeal consonants, for it is hard to see how /H/ could develop to /i/ in Indo-Iranian, but to /a/ independently everywhere else.

[5] W. Cowgill, to whom I am indebted for criticism of an earlier draft of this paper, criticism which has resulted in several major changes of position, objects to this line of argument. He feels that, aside from nouns with no derivative formations entailing *o*-grade (like **ékwos* 'horse') and verbs like **es-* 'to be' which make no perfect tense forms or causatives, there are no cases of nonapophonic */e/ in Indo-European. And that further, Martinet (1953:253–267) has in fact inferred precisely from the fact that nonapophonic [o] is rare in Indo-European save initially, that initial [o] is to be analyzed as */H_3e/-, though clearly */H_1o/ and */H_3o/ are also possibilities. With Cowgill's statement about */e/ I shall have to agree, with the proviso only that I think there must have been cases of nonapophonic */e/ at one time in the history of Indo-European. Any root originally containing nonapophonic */e/, when it appeared in a morphological category which required */o/, was drawn into the */e/ ~ */o/ apophonic relation, and hence ipso facto came to contain apophonic */e/. About */o/ things are not so simple, and I cannot directly answer Cowgill's objection. But

to anticipate my rules concerning IE */a/, and the speculation in Appendix I, I give (provisionally) the following rule which it seems to me will handle IE */o/:

$$*/o/ > \begin{cases} /o/ \text{ when accented} \\ /{:}/ \text{ unaccented after } \begin{bmatrix} i \\ u \end{bmatrix} \\ \emptyset \text{ elsewhere} \end{cases}$$

This rule applies only to nonapophonic */o/, because clearly apophonic */o/ does not pass to Ø when unaccented. It operates to give Skt. *ákṣi* 'eye', Gk. ὄσσε 'eyes (dual)', but Skt. *ī́kṣate* 'sees' (< **i-okʷs-;* cf. M. I.95).

[6] In fact the idea goes back farther than that, but phrased in unacceptable form in terms of a three-vowel (/a i u/), ablaut-governed system. Thus Schleicher (1866:18) gives as the vocalreihe for *a*:

Schwächung	grundvocal	1. steigerung	2. steigerung
i, u; ī, ū	a	ā	ā

He restricted this type of weakening to position before *r*. Examples 1866:21ff.

[7] Hübschmann (1885:3) felt that **agṓ* should give Skt. **ijā́mi.*

[8] Buck (1896:285–286) objected to the number of aorist presents required by Bechtel's hypothesis, for Bechtel would have to assume that: **ágō* < **agṓ* < **āgṓ;* and also to the *-to-* participles *bhaktáḥ* from *bhaj-* (below II.4), *mattáḥ* from *mad-* (below II.25), and also *ajā́* (below I.16), all of which words should by Bechtel's rules show */i/ in the initial syllable in Sanskrit. And Brugmann (1897:173) points to *sthítiḥ* = στάσις as proof that [ə] could appear under the accent, an argument which we shall have to consider below. Buck's first objection, though legitimate and telling against Bechtel's formulation of the rule, will prove to have no bearing on mine. His second does at first glance seem difficult, but the vowel appears in a closed syllable in *bhaktáḥ* and *mattáḥ,* a position which prevented the passage of /a/ to /i/; and both forms have beside them presents with the same grade of the root, and this grade may have been analogically restored to the *-tó-* participle. They would, then, be no more unusual than *spaṣṭáḥ* to *paś-* 'see' (<*(*s*)*peḱtós*) or Gk. πεπτός to πέσσω 'cook' (<**pekʷtós*), Skt. *paktvā́.* About *ajā́* we shall see below.

[9] These forms are taken primarily from Pokorny (777–778). Arm. *amokʻ* 'sweet' and Macedonian ἀβρο- zusammenziehend', Gk. ἀβαρύ · ὀρίγανον (Hes.) are omitted as being too uncertain.

[10] Cf. above note 3 for */o/ > /:/. Again the proviso that the vowel be accented must be added, for IE **yós* 'who (rel.)' appears as Gk. ὅς and Skt. *yaḥ,* not Skt. **īḥ.*

[11] We could omit one step in this development, perhaps thus increasing its plausibility, by assuming that **nro-* passed directly to **anro-*. No other words in Greek would exclude such a development, but the family of ἀνήρ itself seems to stand in the way. For if we assume **nro-* > **anro-,* we deprive ourselves of any possibility of explaining the irregular Homeric scansion of ἀνδροτῆτα (ῠῠ—ῠ: = *ἀροτῆτα?).

[12] But of course if one wishes to restrict the application of the rule to position before semivowels, such is certainly possible. Doing so would at one blow remove all the exceptions to the rule given in the text, and the new rule could be stated:

I-I initial unaccented $/a/ > \emptyset \ \_\_ \begin{bmatrix} i \\ u \end{bmatrix}$, /a/ elsewhere: *ajā́, ajáḥ* (I.16), *amláḥ* (I.11), *argháḥ* (I.13), and *aráḥ* (I.19) will now survive as such because not before semivowel. I do not favor this new rule for two reasons. First, it introduces a certain complexity into an otherwise straightforward rule, since now surrounding phonemes as well as accent are relevant. This is probably not much of a consideration, but more important, *ṛtáḥ* (to *aráḥ* and *áram*) seems to indicate that unaccented /a/ regularly disappeared initially before /r/ as well. This fact indicates that the definition of semivowel would have to be extended to include /r/ if the new formulation is to be retained, but would still exclude /m/. This is not impossible, but even at that *aráḥ* and *argháḥ* are still exceptions, and narrowing the application of the rule only to account for two exceptions does not seem worth it. I favor the broadest possible formulation of the rule, but would not argue too strenuously against the narrower one.

Perhaps at this point *āyúḥ, ā́yu* (I.23), and *āvī́ḥ* (I.24) can be reintroduced and rehabilitated with IE */a/-. The Ave. genitive of *āyū* 'Lebensdauer' is *yaoš,* without initial vowel. It may well be that this ablaut relation points to an original I-I paradigm: **áyus, *ayóus,* which became **áyus, *yóus* as the result of the loss of initial unaccented */a/. At a date posterior to this stage, but still within the I-I period, the accent was removed to the ending in the nominative as well, and the vowel lengthened (vṛdhhied) in order to avoid the loss of */a/-, now unaccented. The long /a:/- was then generalized in Sanskrit to all forms and derivatives of this word, Ave. alone preserving the original genitive. We must then imagine a similar, though unexplained, ablaut relation in Skt. *āvī́ḥ*. This "prophylactic lengthening" which, when involving apophonic /o/, travels under the name of Brugmann's Law, can apply, then, to */a/ as well as to */o/.

[13] Connection between a Skt. word and Lat. *vacca* can still be maintained if we assume that Lat. *vacca* replaces earlier Lat. **vāca,* with gemination replacing length (cf. *lītera* ∼ *littera*), and that Skt. *vāśitā* contains the same word suffixed with *-tā*. We shall see below that internal IE */a/ passes to I-I /i/ when unaccented. Hence on this assumption the IE form will have been */wa:ka/, a form preserved in Latin but extended by *-tā* in Sanskrit. Skt. *vaśā́* might very possibly then be a different remodeling of the original form.

[14] Hitt. *šaša-* (Friedrich 1952:188) is sometimes brought into consideration here, and would of course support my argument by showing that there was an Eastern IE word meaning 'hare' (<**soso-* ?) not connected with Western **ḱas-*. But the meaning of the Hitt. word is not securely established, and hence *šaša-* cannot be used. Friedrich later (1957:18) records Laroche's comparison of this word with the ideogram UDU.KUR.RA in the meaning 'antelope'.

[15] I admit here only those cases which show a correspondence Eur. /a/ = Skt. /i/, and therefore do not include:

Lat. *datus* = Gk. *δοτός* = Skt. *ditaḥ* 'given'
Lat. *factus* = Gk. *θετός* = Skt. *hitaḥ* 'placed'

because the Gk. form does not contain /a/. I want, in other words, to avoid in the text the question of the 'triple reflex of schwa in Greek' (Lejeune 1955:164). There are in fact only two possible explanations for this triple reflex, neither one really affecting my argument at this point. Either Greek preserves the original vocalism and Latin and Sanskrit experienced a merger of unaccented /e/ and /o/ with unaccented /a/ when in disyllables between stop consonants; or Greek has innovated in bringing the timber of the vowel of the strong grade over into the weak grade: on this assumption the original IE forms were **datós* and **dhatós*. I feel that in fact Greek has innovated, but in so doing has recaptured the original form. That is to say I feel that the development of 'placed' was: **[dhetos] > *[dhətos] = /dhatos/ > Skt. *hitaḥ,* Lat. *factus.* (For the notation and presuppositions see Appendix I). Thus I get the best of both worlds, but for the time being at least prefer to exclude cases of this sort from consideration of IE */a/.

16 Brosman's explanation of the origin of *-i* in Hitt. may of course not be correct: -/i/ was added to /r/ and /n/ in Indo-European in other categories as well. In Hitt. itself -/i/ was added to -/r/ in the middle ending *-tari,* as opposed to Lat. *-tur.* And in Vedic Sanskrit the neuter singular of nouns in *-tṛ* is *-tari* (Lanman 1880:421–423). There is also the alternation in the locative singular in Vedic between *rā́jan* and *rā́jani.* It may be that the Hitt. *-i* in the neuter plural has the same origin. The important thing, though, is that, even if this -/i/ be transported as an allomorph of the neuter plural back into Indo-European, it is restricted to *r-* and *n-*stems, and it still remains the case that -/a/ was the vowel added to *nt-*stems.

17 Benveniste (1962:111–112) denies connection of Hitt. *mekki-* with the IE forms in *meg-* because the *-kk-,* according to Sturtevant's rule, points rather to IE */k/ than to */g/, and because the meaning 'viel, sehr' is too distant from 'gross'. He compares the Hitt. word with Toch. *māk* 'viel'. But neither of these objections is enough to destroy the connection (Mayrhofer 1964:194–195), for the semantic difficulty is slight indeed, and there are other exceptions to Sturtevant's rule such as *uqqa* 'ego'.

18 Two other forms have occasionally been considered to contain unaccented I-I /a/:

a) Skt. *kúha,* Ave. *kudā,* OCS *kъde,* Osc. *puf* (cf. Lat. *ali-cubi*) < **kudha* (P. 647, M. I.249, W-H II.739, E-M 716).
b) Skt. *ámba* 'mother (voc.)', Gk. vocatives like *νύμφα* 'maiden' (Wackernagel 1896:6, Pedersen 1900:78–79, Güntert 1916:10–11).

a) The *-ha* in the Skt. form would seem to be the same *-ha* as in *ihá,* and hence to derive from an originally accented -/a/, with secondary shift of accent, in which event it is only apparently a negative instance. And the *-dha* must have originally been something of a free-standing particle. But if one takes the OCS form to heart, one may well conclude that the IE form was **kúdhe,* not *kúdha* (so P.). b) Pedersen introduced *ámba* in support of his contention that IE final */a/ > /a/ in Indo-Iranian. And though it is likely that Skt. voc. /e/ of *a*-stems derives from earlier */ai/ (=/a/ + /i/), *ámba* cannot be used as evidence for voc. -/a/ equatable with Gk. voc. -/a/: it is quite clearly a Lallwort, as Güntert says.

[19] In support of nonphonological conditioning cf. Kiparsky (1967:128): 'Nonphonetic environments in sound change, and the corollary of phonetic doublets in the case of ambiguity, deserve more attention than they usually get. To the extent that they are dealt with at all in the neogrammarian-structuralist tradition of historical linguistics, it is in terms of concepts such as "restressing" or "analogy" which are inadequate to the purpose, as should be apparent from the above examples'. Professor Kiparsky kindly refers me to a massively documented case in which the same phoneme developed in two ways (Lindgren 1953). In Middle High German final *-e* disappeared in certain cases early on, while it was preserved for some time in others: e.g. in the noun *-e* remained as a mark of gender and number distinctions, but disappeared as a case marker (Lindgren 1953:211–225). Since there is no phonemic distinction, the only conditioning must have been functional, i.e. morphological. He also refers me to the case of final *-n* in Estonian. In Estonian Balto-Finnic final *-n* is normally lost, e.g. gen. sg. **kanðan* 'base' (Finn. *kannan*) > Est. *kanna.* But in the first person singular *-n* has remained: **kanðan* 'I carry' (Finn. *kannan*) > Est. *kannan.* The following other cases from the classical languages which may be instances of the same phenomenon occur to me. 1) *-/ewa/ develops in two ways in Attic Greek depending on whether it is the ending of the neuter plural of a noun or of an adjective: */ástewa/ 'cities' > ἄστη, but */hɛ:déwa/ 'sweet' > ἡδέα. 2) Though the spiritus asper is regularly preserved in Locrian (and other forms of) Greek, it is lost in the definite article (Buck 1955:53–54). 3) IE */ty/ develops in two ways in certain forms of Greek depending on whether the */y/ formed part of a derivative suffix based on Gk. material, or whether the form was unmotivated from the Gk. point of view (Lejeune 1955:87–88, Buck 1955:69–71). 4) IE */o:/ develops in Umbrian to /u/ in the ablative singular of *o*-stems and in imperatives (<*/o:d/), but to /o/ in the genitive plural of *o*-stems (<*/o:m/) and elsewhere (Poultney 1959:36–37). Doubtless other explanations can be conceived of to account for these divergent developments—accent in 1) and 2), chronological layers in 3), phonetic environment in 4)—, but grammatical interference seems at present the best one.

[20] The -/a/ in these forms, then, may well have had the same function as the -/a/ in Gk. interjections (σίττα, ψίττα) and names of letters of the alphabet (ἄλφα, βῆτα) for *st! pst!* and *aleph*, *bēt* respectively (Schwyzer 1931). In all these cases the addition of -/a/ was the alternative to phonotactic loss of final consonant.

[21] Still another possibility of an explanation is that at the time that unaccented

-/a/ was passing to [ə], the endings of the perfect were accented and hence unaffected. In this event the perfect paradigm would have been : ***widá* ***witsthá* ***widé,* which later, with the introduction of /o/ became PIE **wóida* **wóitstha* **wóide.* On this possibility and the theoretical framework underlying it, see below Appendix II, and also, with a different theoretical base, Schmitt-Brandt (1967: 124–125).

22 Cases involving vowels other than /a/ include:

/o/ Skt. *ánīkam* 'face, front' < **eni* + *ok*^{w}-, Gk. ἐνωπή 'face' (M. I.34).
Skt. *abhīke* 'immediately before' < **abhi* + *ok*^{w}- (M. I.42).
Skt. *prátīkam* 'surface' < **proti* + *ok*^{w}-, Gk. πρόσωπον 'face' (M. II.361).
/e/ Skt. *apīcyaḥ* 'secret, hidden' < **epi* + *enk*^{w}- (M. I.39).

23 Some such development together with this resulting system is customarily assumed. The difference between my view and older views is that I do not assume that unaccented long vowels appear as schwa, an assumption shared by most laryngealists and the more traditional Indo-Europeanists. But it is clear that unaccented long vowels are not reduced (cf. Gk. ἡδύς 'sweet', Skt. *svādúḥ* 'id.'), and it would be most surprising (theoretically) if they were. Again one may compare Latin, a language in which internal short vowels were shortened or raised (as in *animus* < **anemos* or **anamos*), but in which long vowels were unaffected (cf. *amārus*).

24 I thus agree with Schmitt-Brandt (1966, 1967:8–31), and also with Skt. grammarians, in positing the so-called reduced grade of the root as the basic form of the root, at least in those roots which contained a semivowel. I cannot, however, subscribe to Schmitt-Brandt's speculations concerning still earlier stages of Indo-European.

25 In this way I hope to forestall the plausible objection to my theory raised by Cowgill. He finds it difficult to accept that unaccented /a/ > [ə] > I-I /i/, while /e/ remains /e/ whether accented or not: he feels that if /a/ > /i/, then /e/ should be affected as well. The answer is to be sought in relative chronology. At the time that /a/ > [ə], /e/ > Ø, but after the accent shift (both in syllable accented and in type of accent) there was no further syncope of short vowels.

26 My position involves me in certain predictions, and though it is the case that their nonfulfillment will not invalidate the theory, their fulfillment will provide a measure of support for it. Using /i/ to represent both /i/ and /u/, /e/ to represent both /e/ and /o/, we should find the following restrictions on the occurrence of stem shapes. /é/ should occur anywhere, while /è/ (unaccented /e/) should occur only in those stems which also contain /é/: sigla *CèCé-* or *CéCè-*, for every /è/ is a former /é/, except in the case of analogically introduced /è/ as in thematic present endings. *CèCé-* must derive from *CéC-*, while *CéCè-* derives from *CCé-:* the accented vowel is the more recently introduced one. /í/ should not occur in ablauting paradigms, since /í/ was always replaced by /éi/. Nor should /á/ occur, save in the first syllable of the imperfective of a root

which had at one time appeared as *CaCé-*, as in the thematic (second) aorist. Otherwise original /a/ appeared as either *CéCà-* < *CCá-* or as *CéaC-* (>*Ca*:*C*- or *Co*:*C*-, depending on whether /e/ was a front vowel or a back vowel) <*CáC-*; or as *CCéa-*, if from *CCá-*. That these predictions in fact are frequently realized is corroborative of my view, but it must in fairness be admitted that the older theories of ablaut make many of the same predictions.

References

Bartholomae, Christian

1895 Vorgeschichte der iranischen Sprachen. Grundriss der Iranischen Philologie. Hrsg. W. Geiger & E. Kuhn. Vol. I.1–151. Strassburg.

Bechtel, Fritz

1892 Die Hauptprobleme der indogermanischen Lautlehre seit Schleicher. Göttingen.

Benveniste, Émile

1962 Hittite et Indo-Européen: Études comparatives. Paris.

Birwé, Robert

1956 Review of M. I.I–XXV, 1–128, in IF 62:195–200.

Brosman, Paul W.

1962 Neuter Plural in *-i* among Hittite Consonant Stems. JAOS 82:63–65.

Brugmann, Karl

1876 Nasalis sonans in der indogermanische Grundsprache. Curtius Studien 9:285–328.

1904 Kurze vergleichende Grammatik der indogermanischen Sprachen. Berlin.

1897 Grundriss der vergleichenden Grammatik der indogermanischen Sprachen. Vol. I pt. 1: Einleitung und Lautlehre. 2d ed. Strassburg.

1911 *Op. cit.* Vol. II pt. 2: Lehre von den Wortformen und ihrem Gebrauch. 2d ed. Strassburg.

Buck, Carl Darling

1896 Some General Problems of Ablaut. American Journal of Philology 17:267–288.

1955 The Greek Dialects. Chicago.

Burrow, T.
1946 Loanwords in Sanskrit. Transactions of the Philological Society 1–30.
1949 "Schwa" in Sanskrit. Transactions of the Philological Society 22–61.
1955 The Sanskrit Language. London.

Cardona, George
1961 Greek *kámnō* and *támnō*. Language 36:502–507.

Friedrich, Johannes
1952 Hethitisches Wörterbuch. Heidelberg.
1957 Hethitisches Wörterbuch I. Ergänzungsheft. Heidelberg.

Frisk, Hjalmar
1934 Zur Indoiranischen und Griechischen Nominalbildung. Göteborgs Kungl. Vetenskaps- och Vitterhets-Samhälles Handlingar, V A 4 nr. 4. Göteborg.
1938 Indogermanica (=Göteborgs Högskolas Årsskrift 44 nr. 1). Göteborg.

Guntert, Hermann
1916 Indogermanische Ablautprobleme. Strassburg.

Hirt, Hermann
1900 Der indogermanische Ablaut. Strassburg.
1928 Indogermanische Grammatik. Vol. IV: Doppelung, Zusammensetzung, Verbum. Heidelberg.

Hübschmann, Heinrich
1885 *Das indogermanische Vokalsystem.* Strassburg.
1900 Review of Hirt 1900, in IF Anzeiger 11:24–56.

Kiparsky, Paul
1967 A Phonological Rule of Greek. Glotta 44:109–134.

Krahe, Hans
1962 Indogermanische Sprachwissenschaft. Vol. I. Berlin

Kurylowicz, Jerzy
1956 L'apophonie en indo-européen. Wrocław.
1958 L'accentuation des langues indo-européennes. 2d ed. Wrocław.
1958a New Discoveries in Indo-European Studies: a. Le Hittite. In Proceedings of the VIII International Congress of Linguists. Oslo.
1962 Probleme der indogermanischen Lautlehre. II Fachtagung für indogermanische und allgemeine Sprachwissenschaft. J. Knobloch, ed. (Innsbrucker Beiträge zur Kulturwissenschaft 15.) Innsbruck.

LANMAN, CHARLES R.
1880 A Statistical Account of Noun-Inflection in the Veda. JAOS 10:325–601.

LEJEUNE, MICHEL
1955 Traité de phonétique grecque. 2d ed. Paris.

LINDGREN, KAJ
1953 Die Apokope des MHD *-e* in seinen verschiedenen Funktionen (= Annales Academiae Scientiarum Fennicae B 78:2). Helsinki.

MARTINET, ANDRÉ
1953 Non-Apophonic O-Vocalism in Indo-European. Word 9:253–267. Reprinted in French trans. in Économie des changements phonétiques 212–234. Berne, 1955.

MAYRHOFER, MANFRED
1952 Das Gutturalproblem und das indogermanische Wort für "Hase". Studien zur indogermanischen Grundsprache 27–32. Hrsg. v. W. Brandenstein (Arbeiten aus dem Institut für allg. u. vgl. Sprachwissenschaft 4). Graz.
1964 Review of Benveniste 1962, in Die Sprache 10:174–197.

PALMER, LEONARD R.
1961 The Latin Language. Third Impression. London.

PEDERSEN, HOLGER
1900 Wie viel Laute gab es im Indogermanischen. KZ 36:74–110.
1905 Die nasalpräsentia und der slavische akzent. KZ 38:297–421.
1907 Die idg.-semitische Hypothese und die idg. Lautlehre. IF 22:341–365.
1909 Vergleichende Grammatik der keltischen Sprachen. Vol. I: Einleitung und Lautlehre. Göttingen.
1926 La cinquième déclinaison latine (= Det Kongelige Danske Videnskabernes Selskab. Historisk-Filologiske Meddelelser XI:5). Copenhagen.
1931 Linguistic Science in the Nineteenth Century. Trans. J. W. Spargo. Cambridge.

POLOMÉ, EDGAR G. C.
1965 The Laryngeal Theory So Far: A Critical Bibliographical Survey. Evidence for Laryngeals 9–78. W. Winter, ed. The Hague.

POULTNEY, JAMES W.
1959 The Bronze Tables of Iguvium (= American Philological Association Monographs 18). Baltimore.

PUHVEL, JAAN

1964 A Mycenaean-Vedic titular coincidence. KZ 79:1–7.

RENOU, LOUIS

1964 Védique *sādh-, khād-* et *śās-*. Indo-Iranica 163–167. Mélanges présentés à Georg Morgenstierne. Wiesbaden.

SAUSSURE, FERDINAND DE

1879 Mémoire sur le système primitif des voyelles dans les langues indo-européennes. Leipzig. Cited by page number in Saussure, 1922.

1922 Recueil des publications scientifiques. Geneva.

SCHLEICHER, AUGUST

1866 Compendium der vergleichenden grammatik der indogermanischen Sprachen. 2d ed. Weimar.

SCHMIDT, JOHANNES

1889 Die Pluralbildungen der indogermanischen Neutra. Weimar.

SCHMITT-BRANDT, ROBERT

1966 Probleme des indogermanischen Vokalismus. Kratylos 11:166–174.

1967 Die Entwicklung des indogermanischen Vokalsystems. Heidelberg.

SCHWYZER, EDUARD

1932 Neugriech. *βέσσα* (Chios), altgriech. *βῆσσα* und Verwandtes. Rheinisches Museum 88:193–203.

1931 Griechische Interjektionen und griechische Buchstabennamen auf *-a*. KZ 58:170–203.

1939 Griechische Grammatik. Vol. I. Munich.

STREITBERG, W.

1915 Ferdinand de Saussure. Indogermanisches Jahrbuch 2:203–213.

SZEMERÉNYI, OSWALD J. L.

1952 The Etymology of German *Adel*. Word 8:42–50.

1960 The Origin of Greek *βαθύς* and *βόθυνος*. Glotta 38:211–216.

1964 Structuralism and Substratum—Indo-Europeans and Aryans in the Ancient Near East. Lingua 13:1–29.

1964a Syncope in Greek and Indo-European and the Nature of Indo-European Accent (=Instituto universitario orientale di Napoli, Quaderni della sezione linguistica degli annali 3). Naples.

1967 The New Look of Indo-European—Reconstruction and Typology. Phonetica 17:65–99.

THIEME, PAUL
1953 Die Heimat der indogermanischen Gemeinsprache (=Abhandlungen der Geistes- und Sozialwissenschaftlichen Klasse, Akademie der Wissenschaften und der Literatur. 11:535–613. Mainz.
1955 Review of Burrow 1956. Language 31:428–456.

WACKERNAGEL, JAKOB
1888 Miszellen zur griechischen Grammatik: 14. ἕκαστος. KZ 29:144–151 (=Kleine Schriften 647–654). Göttingen.
1896 Altindische Grammatik. Vol. I: Lautlehre. Göttingen.
1905 *Op. cit.* Vol. II.1: Einleitung zur Wortlehre. Nominalkomposition. Göttingen.
1954 *Op. cit.* Vol. II.2: Die Nominalsuffixe (by Albert Debrunner). Göttingen.

WYATT, WILLIAM F., JR.
1964 Structural Linguistics and the Laryngeal Theory. Language 40:138–152.

DATE DUE

~~NO 1 '70~~			
~~JE 6 '72~~			
SEP 22 1973			
DE 12 '75			

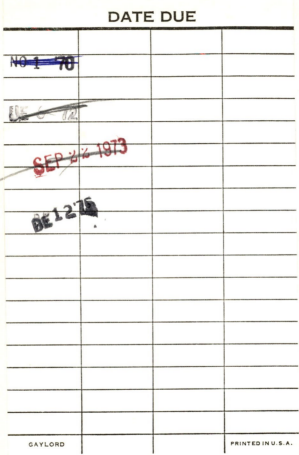